This is a searing and ultimately beautiful story of Kathy Izard's years-long pilgrimage on the knife-edge of time and eternity. It speaks to all who want to find a path of faith, to a life worth living, and a love worth living with.

—LEIGHTON FORD, Founding President, Leighton Ford Ministries, author of *The Attentive Life, Transforming Leadership, The Power of Story* and *Sandy: A Heart for God.*

Reading *The Last Ordinary Hour* feels like listening to that friend who trusts you with her deepest secrets. Kathy Izard shares how she chose to live with grace instead of fear when her husband's precarious medical condition could not be fixed. When Dr. Google scares you and no amount of money will cure you, this book holds your hand and heals your soul.

—JUDY SELDIN-COHEN, author of *Recharging Judaism*

Honest and open, Kathy Izard has penned a gift to anyone wondering how to journey on and fully love and embrace a life they never planned or imaged. With the fear she could become a widow at any moment, Kathy takes us on a journey of awakening to, and truly living, the life we've been dealt, and invites us to make it our own. *The Last Ordinary Hour* is a book I'll read and reread. It's a book I didn't know I was waiting for.

—NIKI HARDY, author of *Breathe Again*, host of the podcast *Chemo Chair Prayers* and *The Trusting God Through Cancer Summit*

This deeply moving story describes Kathy's journey through shock, recovery, and healing into thriving—together with her husband. It is an incredible read that I could not put down. And her weaving of quotes from authors like Frederick Buechner, Barbara Brown Taylor, Rachel Held Evans, and Richard Rohr paralleled my own faith journey. Highly recommended!

—BRIAN ALLAIN, Founder of Writing for Your Life, Publishing in Color, Compassionate Christianity, and How to Heal Our Divides

In reading Kathy Izard's *The Last Ordinary Hour*, I frequently found myself looking up to see if the earth had shifted or just my way of thinking. The author's prose is fierce and unflinching. Just like the beloved labyrinths that she encounters, the reader will gladly go through all the medical twists and turns that confront Ms. Izard and her husband. After finishing *The Last Ordinary Hour*, I dare the reader to not ask themselves "What are you going to do with your one wild and precious life?"

—LESLIE HOOTON, author of *Before Anyone Else* and *The Secret of Rainy Days*

Kathy Izard takes you by the hand and invites you to accompany her on an incredible journey. Through the darkest of hours to an inspiring opening of her heart and soul, she reveals tender and vulnerable parts of herself that draw you close. Throughout the book she weaves the wisdom of other seekers, but the most poignant wisdom comes from her own deep and authentically earned perspective. *The Last Ordinary Hour* is a must-read for those who have suffered tragedy and loss, for those who seek to deepen spiritual life, and also for readers who simply long for a book you just can't put down.

—KATHERINE OLIVETTI, MA, MSSW, author of *The Guided Dream Journal*

Kathy Izard's powerful story is deeply personal, and it also contains questions we all face. How do we live in faith not fear? How do we love when we know we risk losing? Kathy's experiences and insights show us that even when we can no longer cling to a straightforward "plan," we can keep taking the next, Spirit-led step forward on the path. This beautiful, compelling book is a powerful love story and an astute exploration of what it means to have faith when the future is entirely uncertain.

—KATE H. RADEMACHER, author of *Reclaiming Rest* and *Their Faces Shone*

The Last Ordinary Hour is a kind and generous guide for anyone who has ever stood at the edge of their own abyss or worried how they would survive if faced with doing so. It is also for anyone who has felt called to go deeper on the spiritual journey and wondered how to begin.

—JULIE MARR, Spiritual Director and Founder, Soul School

In *The Last Ordinary Hour*, Kathy Izard has captured the quicksand of uncertainty that consumes a SCAD patient's family while navigating this complex, devastating diagnosis full of unknowns and heartache. Also a one-of-a-kind love story, *The Last Ordinary Hour* shows us we can thrive even in the most challenging times.

—KATHERINE LEON, Founder and Chair, SCAD Alliance

This book will stop and start your heart several times. Not because it is scary but because it is sacred. Kathy Izard, well known as an advocate for the homeless, shares what she calls her "spiritual homelessness" when her heli-skiing, highly successful, Mickey Mouse–pancake-flipping dad to their four daughters, almost dies a few times, *does* die once, and manages not to make her a widow. Alongside their story, she strings together pearls from the mountain of books she has read while on a quest to make sense of suffering, random bad luck and faith in a loving God. Readers will not wish for a spouse as sick as Kathy's, but they will wish for a marriage, and a spiritual homecoming, like hers.

—REVEREND LISA G. SAUNDERS, author of *Even at the Grave*

THE

LAST

ORDINARY

HOUR

ALSO BY
KATHY IZARD

THE HUNDRED STORY HOME
A Memoir of Finding Faith in Ourselves
and Something Bigger

A GOOD NIGHT
FOR MR. COLEMAN

THE
LAST
ORDINARY
HOUR

LIVING LIFE

NOW THAT NOTHING

WILL EVER BE

THE SAME

KATHY IZARD

grace press
NORTH CAROLINA

Grace Press, LLC
1717 Cleveland Avenue
Charlotte, NC 28203

www.kathyizard.com

FIRST PAPERBACK EDITION MAY 2021

Book cover design by Jon Valk
Book interior design by Karen Minster
Proofreading by Debra Nichols
Editing by Elizabeth Dickens
Author photo by Julia Fay Photography

ISBN 978-0-9977784-3-4 (paperback)
ISBN 978-0-9977784-4-1 (ebook)

FOR DR. JANE

With gratitude for all you have done and continue to do
to save and encourage the one heart most dear to me.

And for making me believe in
all the angels among us and above us.

———

Now faith is the assurance of things hoped for,
the conviction of things not seen.

HEBREWS 11:1

CONTENTS

AUTHOR'S NOTE

While our four daughters are very much a part of our lives and these events, their presence in these pages is intentionally limited. As an author I write about what happened to me in hopes of helping others, but as a mother I am protective of stories that are not mine to tell.

PROLOGUE

It wasn't until seven years after it happened that I could see it for what it was. At the time, it just felt like I had unwillingly crossed a threshold, which plunged me into an inescapable abyss. As if I had been walking along unsuspecting in a field and tumbled into an abandoned mine shaft. The more I tried to claw my way out, the more futile it became as the sides slipped and crumbled beneath my grasp.

I had no choice but to remain in that dark place. Eventually, I began moving toward light—not sunlight but moonlight. It illuminated my path just enough so that I could put one foot in front of the other. Most days, that dimly lit world felt like a maze with one dead end after another. At times the path made me feel like I was moving forward only to inexplicably circle back. Just when I thought I would never reach the end, the way revealed itself.

I would come to learn I was not in a maze or even a hole. I had never been lost. I was learning to be found. I was on an inner journey to discover myself. That path inward is not a maze—it's a labyrinth. An ancient sacred path seemingly unmarked and maddeningly obscure but in reality, one that takes only an inkling of faith to find. To reach the center of your soul simply requires trusting the twists and believing in the destination.

A labyrinth is intentionally designed to bring you to the center of yourself and then lead you back into the world with gems of wisdom. Although you travel the same path each journey inward, you will glean a different message each time. There is a pattern to this collecting and building knowledge: releasing, receiving, returning. Each time you enter a labyrinth anew, you must release your old ideas. It will feel unsettling to let go of what you believe to be true and you will want to step off the path, choose an easier or more direct route, or hurry the process. But if you remain steady, trusting the sacred way, you will always *arrive at the center. Here, you receive and understand the truth of your journey. Cradling this new knowledge, you return to your world, retracing your steps in a mirror image of how you arrived yet always transformed from how you began.*

Once you have found the entrance, you can never lose your way again. In each difficult time, you can revisit this place of comfort seeking solace and asking for new truths to be revealed following this same ritual: releasing, receiving, returning. This most important journey we travel is never outside the world, it is accessing the divine always present inside ourselves.

For years I believed I was wandering, but, in reality, I was preparing. Nothing I had done and no steps I had taken earlier were unnecessary. They were all exactly as they needed to be to find my own entrance at exactly the right time. Enter this sacred threshold too soon and you might dismiss the significance of your discovery. Cross without reverence and you might exit too quickly. But once you are truly ready for your inner walk, you cannot miss the signs clearly guiding you out of your own abyss.

Those holes we plunge into are not malicious—they are intentional. They appear once we are ready to understand all we have come here to do. The lessons we need to learn, they never happen in the light. They always happen in the dark. We can't become who we were meant to be admiring ourselves in the mirror. Our true selves are revealed and our innate strength is developed when we are on our knees—keenly aware that we are not God and fully understanding how much we need faith to survive.

SHATTERING

THE WISH FOR THE CURE IS SEDUCTIVE; it captivates and charms. Devastating illness, despite its ability to utterly transform, is not revered in the same way. Illness is viewed as an aberrant state. It is a town we drive through on a journey home, but not a place to stop and linger. We pass through with gritted teeth, as if it were a storm, with no regard for the illuminating beauty of the lightning as it strikes. But those shattering moments that break our bodies also allow us to access wisdom that is normally hidden, except in times of utter darkness.

DR. RANA AWDISH

In Shock: My Journey from Death to Recovery
and the Redemptive Power of Hope

1

BREAKING

THE MOMENT WE
NEVER SEE COMING

If I had to pick a moment, one moment where normal morphed into surreal, I would have to say it began with a turkey sandwich in a quaint New England café seven states away from where my husband, Charlie, and I call home. Our parents weekend in Massachusetts did not seem exotic or dangerous. We had traveled often to destinations intentionally selected for the lack of cell service and rugged remoteness. Over the past ten years, we vacationed with our four daughters in places I had specifically chosen so that Charlie's cell-phone screen would read "No Service" and where his ever-present work would have to wait.

It was a chilly February Friday and we had taken our daughter, Emma, to lunch at a cozy New England café. We all ordered turkey sandwiches and during lunch we had discussed the weather (snowy) and Emma's mood (nervous). We delivered Emma back to campus and hugged her good-bye with promises to see her after the play. At the time, we absolutely believed we would. The fact that our lives were about to change forever simply had not occurred to any of us.

Returning to the hotel, Charlie had predictably gone to the gym and I had, equally predictably, chosen to answer emails rather than exercise. My husband, once a two-time All-American lacrosse player, worked out religiously while I regularly avoided the gym. I was still intent on my inbox, comfortably curled up on the gray-suede sofa in our hotel room when Charlie uncharacteristically returned from the fitness room after only twenty minutes.

Opening our hotel room door, Charlie shuffled past me, clutching his upper arms in obvious distress. Normally, he stands six feet, four inches and he maintains his fit, fifty-three-year-old frame through rigorous workouts, which always involve intense sweating. Now hunched over in some kind of obvious pain, Charlie seemed at least ten inches shorter. His brown hair was still perfectly in place with no perspiration and his faded gray Nike T-shirt was completely devoid of any signs of sweat. Charlie fell heavily onto the stiff hotel mattress with his right hand resting on his chest. He spoke softly to no one in particular, "I am so tired. I think I will take a nap."

With his eyes closed, Charlie rested only ten feet away and his impossibly long legs were hanging over the side of the bed not quite touching the floor. He had landed short of the pillows so his head was not elevated and his body was sprawled diagonally across the bed in an uncomfortable-looking position. Studying him from the couch, I was perplexed but not alarmed. Along with his dutiful daily exercise, Charlie maintained 200 pounds of lean muscle with a diet any doctor would have approved. Boneless grilled chicken with steamed vegetables was his preferred dinner and chocolate chip cookies were his only vice.

Although his days as a collegiate athlete were long over, Charlie remained dedicated to training and playing all kinds of sports. He had even grown to love adrenalin-inducing exploits like heli-skiing. The past three winters Charlie had jumped off cliffs in Canada, and he came home each time dedicated to returning the next year. Relaxing was not a concept that resonated with Charlie. He pushed through punishing workouts even after long days at the office. His weekends were a marathon of activity—running, golf, tennis, and hiking.

During recent workouts, however, Charlie had noticed mild chest and arm pain so his general practitioner had referred him to a cardiologist. Charlie's diagnostic stress test on a treadmill was almost laughable. In a medical office environment, they could barely get Charlie's heart rate above 100 beats per minute because he was in such exceptional shape. After several visits over five months, the cardiologist was confident there was no cause for concern. The diagnosis was simply "stress." There were no suggestions for an improved diet or fitness regimen—just the advice to try to work less to reduce his stress. Charlie had waved that one off. He didn't roll that way.

So, while I was surprised that Charlie would ever leave a gym before finishing his workout, I was not concerned. Whatever this unusual behavior was, it couldn't be cardiac related. Maybe he was just a little jet-lagged. In the past thirty-six hours, Charlie had unpacked bags from a beach trip where we had vacationed with friends, repacked to fly to Boston for a series of meetings before finally making the drive to attend Emma's play.

Abandoning my computer and endless emails, I stood up to get a closer look at Charlie. Although his face and forearms were still impressively tanned from the beach, his hands were white—ghostly in fact—as if no blood were circulating beneath the skin. My heart started beating a little quicker. I had no medical training but I knew this lack of color in his extremities could not be considered normal.

My brain began to race. Did he need an ambulance? Should I dial 911?

Maybe I should just drive him somewhere. On the way to our hotel, I remembered seeing a bright-orange sign for a new emergency clinic about five to ten minutes away.

"Charlie, I know you don't want to overreact, but I think we need to go the urgent care."

He didn't respond. My pulse picked up. I tried again, this time with authority in my voice.

"Charlie, get up. We are going to the clinic," I commanded, hoping he would comply.

Charlie began to stir but his eyes remained closed as he struggled to sit up. He moved as if sleepwalking out of our room, into the elevator and finally, into the rental car. As I Googled for directions, Charlie's sluggish steps accelerated my panic. What could be causing this? Charlie appeared drunk and exhausted.

As I drove the unfamiliar, snow-packed, small-town streets, I monitored Charlie with sideways glances. With his eyes pressed closed, Charlie remained slumped in the passenger seat and continued to cradle his chest with both hands. "I think you better drive faster," he finally whispered.

The seven-minute car ride felt like seven days. Stumbling into the door of the clinic, Charlie kept clutching his upper arms with his still-white hands. The staff moved slowly at first, Charlie's presenting physical condition delaying any immediate concern. There was no blood to stem, no broken bone to set, no traumatic wound. Just a handsome man moving slowly, complaining of arm pain and chest pressure. To the casual observer, his only obvious symptom appeared to be fatigue and a loss of color. At first glance, maybe the nurse thought Charlie had pulled a muscle or was suffering from severe acid reflux. But she didn't know him. She didn't understand that her patient was a man who never stopped moving, and was now incapacitated from some unknown distress. Charlie had slowed to a crawl as if trapped in quicksand.

As Charlie rested semiconscious on an examination table, the urgent-care staff diligently began their standard checks. Temperature. Blood pressure. Stethoscope. Then suddenly, an EKG machine was whisked in and Charlie was transferred to a mobile bed with side rails. With that, all the rhythms in the room began to pick up speed as if the medical train was leaving the station. A doctor appeared from behind the curtain. Charlie still wasn't speaking and although I was in the cramped bay as well, no one was talking to me. The staff had their own language that consisted not of words but of protocols, which were being performed at an increasingly rapid pace. Their professionalism masked any emotion but they all seemed to know something I didn't.

Had it been merely minutes since we arrived? I had lost track of time but suddenly, we were moving. Everyone was moving. Charlie was unmoving, yet hurrying past me on the gurney. As he rolled away, a nurse shoved his jacket into my arms as she said. "The ambulance is waiting—go!"

Ambulance? When had they called an ambulance?

Still not understanding what was happening, I stumbled toward the back of the waiting emergency vehicle that had magically appeared in the parking lot behind the urgent-care building. Charlie was already being lifted into the back bay. When I tried to climb up beside him, the attending EM stopped me. "Not here—in front," he said motioning with his head toward the cab.

Panicked, I tried to get one reassuring look at Charlie amid all the equipment, but the EMT slammed the metal doors in my face. Taking the passenger seat next to the uniformed driver, I barely had time to close the door before he started the engine.

"Seat belt," he commanded.

The ambulance sped forward in a cacophony of sound which screamed at moving cars to get out of our way. The flashing red lights and screeching sirens warned all the other drivers of the medical drama inside our vehicle but I felt completely unprepared. Nothing had warned me or Charlie that this traumatic out-of-town emergency might occur.

"We are going to the hospital for a test?" I asked, realizing I still was not sure what was happening to Charlie, who, until an hour ago, was the healthiest person I knew.

The driver connected with only the briefest eye contact before once again turning his full attention to the road. But in that glance, I caught a moment of surprise mixed with pity.

"Yes," he said slowly, as if speaking to me in a new language. "A test."

As we arrived at the back of what looked to be a large hospital, I felt I had landed in an episode of *Grey's Anatomy*. Climbing down from passenger seat, I hurried around back but the doors had already been flung open by a waiting trauma team who were not actors. At the center of this drama was my real-life husband. I could barely see his body through the swarming sea of blue scrubs. They all seemed to know exactly what role they were playing. But I still didn't understand mine.

With a blue surgical mask pulled down to his chin, a doctor stepped around the confusion. He seemed to be searching for me. Hours ago, Charlie and this doctor might have stood side by side with similarly tall height and strong build. Now, Charlie appeared small and fragile on the gurney, now swarmed by the waiting hospital staff. The doctor approached me stooping to speak over the commotion.

"Are you the wife?" he asked.

The doctor's matching blue surgeon's cap hid the color of his hair, but bushy black eyebrows hovered over kind brown eyes.

Unable to answer, I nodded, watching as Charlie rolled away from me into a long fluorescent hallway. The silent white walls were a stark contrast to the screeching, flashing red lights of the harrowing ambulance ride.

"Yes, I am his wife, Kathy," I answered before realizing this doctor probably didn't even know his incoming patient's name. "That's Charlie. My husband's name is Charlie."

The doctor nodded but he didn't seem to need either of our names. "Who's your doctor?"

"Doctor?" His question confused me. "We don't have one? We are visiting—we are not from here."

"You are not from here?" The doctor's face registered alarm but he quickly recovered his professionalism. Gazing directly into my eyes, he spoke clear words which were meant to be kind but were shocking, "Your husband's main artery is blocked. We don't have much time. I am going in now."

I had no idea what he meant. *What main artery? Going in where?*

It didn't matter because the doctor wasn't taking questions. Quickly turning away from me, he used his elbows to push through gray metal doors to our left and disappeared. The rising panic from the ambulance ride now morphed into full terror. Twenty feet down the hall, the top of Charlie's chestnut head was barely visible and threatened to disappear forever. Running to catch up, I pushed my way through the trauma team and grabbed Charlie's right hand. Stooping low to whisper in his right ear, I choked on the only words that came to me, "I love you, Goose."

Goose. Because geese mate for life. Because we had married twenty-seven years ago and I couldn't imagine living this life without him. If he heard me, I couldn't say. Charlie's hand slipped from mine as the doors to surgery closed between us.

From behind, a nurse gently pulled me back, guiding me to a waiting room and turning on the lights before rushing away. The room had over forty blue-and-gray colored chairs but no one was seated in them. Completely alone, I collapsed in shock.

How did we go from café to hotel to urgent care to ambulance in under sixty minutes? I didn't even know what hospital we were in and there was no one to ask. While there was a receptionist desk, no one was on duty. Even the mounted television was dark. Wherever we were had already closed for the day and, seemingly, reopened just for us. For Charlie.

In the hallway outside the waiting room, a janitor pushed a broom with solemn, steady strokes as if he had been trained not to disturb. I wanted to do something but I had no idea what I should be doing.

The urge to call someone was overwhelming but I only had 10% battery left and I still had no idea what was happening or who needed to know.

My heart raced. It was not enough, I thought. It was not enough. My cell. The battery. Charlie. It was all not enough. Not enough power. Not enough time. Even if I could call someone, the only person I wanted to talk to was Charlie, my love-at-first-sight soul mate. I wanted to call him and say, "The craziest thing? We were eating lunch and now, you are not here, and I don't want to imagine that you might not ever be here again."

Folding my hands in my lap, I stared at the clock facing me on the wall. It was a round, institutional, standard timekeeper simply displaying the hour, but I could not make sense of the time. There was the time before Charlie collapsed on the hotel bed, seemingly exhausted from a workout, and then, the time after where he lay unconscious on a stretcher. And now, all time was suspended as I waited and worried and wondered.

What was happening in there? Is that guy a good doctor? I don't even know what kind of doctor he is. Where did he go to med school?

The clock kept ticking, ticking. I kept thinking, thinking.

If he was going for a test, why was everyone suited up for surgery?

I told him I loved him but did I kiss him goodbye?

Ticking, ticking. Thinking, thinking.

Why is this taking so long?

Are you fighting, Charlie? Are you fighting to stay here?

Stay with me. Please don't go. You can't go. You can't leave me here. Don't leave me here. Don't leave us here. Us. The girls. Oh my God, the girls.

Crying, crying. Praying, praying.

Dear God. I don't even know what I am praying for because I don't even know what's wrong, but please don't take Charlie. I need him. The girls need him. I can't lose him now. It's too soon.

We need more time. There will never be enough time.

She was a nurse. I could tell that the woman, who was trying to talk with me, was a surgical nurse, because she was wearing the same blue scrubs as the doctor who had met me when we arrived.

As if to soften her look, she had removed her cap but some soft strands from her brown ponytail fell across her face. She looked kind and she looked like she needed me to understand what she was saying, but, at first, I wasn't sure she was speaking English. Her words sounded unintelligible and I know I was not comprehending.

"Your husband," she began, "Your husband has had a heart attack . . ."

"What?" I interrupted shaking my head.

How could Charlie, the healthiest person anyone knew, cleared in a checkup only weeks ago, have had a heart attack? I didn't understand how she could be saying that.

I had been with him in the hotel and the urgent care and the ambulance.

So when did he have a heart attack? Did it happen during his test? Whatever test they ran did it somehow cause a heart attack?

"When did he have a heart attack?" I asked.

She looked at me curiously. "Don't you know that is why you are here?"

I couldn't answer. Is that why no one had explained where we were going?

The nurse reached for my hands, holding them in hers as if we were about to pray together, and delivered her news in slow, soft syllables.

"Your husband's main artery, it's called the LAD, left anterior descending artery, was blocked and it caused a heart attack," she said and waited a moment for me to absorb the news.

"We are not yet sure why it happened but you are very lucky that Dr. Ali was on call—he is the best. He was able to put two stents in your husband's heart. We think he is going to make it."

That was the beginning of a new time zone for us—started by a rare and raw event I never expected, but when it happened, it altered time. There was the time before. And all time after.

I didn't know that day was the beginning of a seven-year walk on a road we could not begin to imagine. I didn't know that it would not be the only time, just the first time, Charlie's incredibly fit and muscled body would fail him. I didn't know that what happened that day wasn't a conventional heart attack but a condition so uncommon in the cardiac world that Charlie would become one of only ten males in a global medical study. I didn't know that living with the minute-by-minute uncertainty of Charlie's health would force me to explore a different kind of certainty about God. And I didn't know that those seven years mired in worry about becoming a widow, were the wake-up call I needed to find a different way to live in faith not fear.

Real faith. Not the kind of faith that suggests there is a God far away in the heavens but the kind of faith that affirms there is a God truly present with us every day on this earth. The kind of faith that teaches me our bodies, which can feel so mundane, are in fact, marvelously made. The kind of faith where I have witnessed that there is a divine current of grace running through this world connecting us to each other and healing us all.

That first time I ended up in the cardiac catheterization waiting room, hearing that Charlie *might* survive, I didn't know or believe any of that. I just thought it was the worst day of my life and the last hour I would ever consider normal. And I didn't yet believe that Charlie's story, our story, was about living. That day, I believed our story was only about not dying.

Today, all the reasons I believe in God have less to do with Charlie's incredible survival than my own journey alongside him. Our two hearts are bound in such a way that when one stops beating, the other will break. For this, there will never be a cure.

It is precisely through this loving and the risk of losing, however, that we are most able to come alive to our own possibilities. After seven years of long nights spent watching Charlie's chest move up and down, willing his heart to keep beating so that mine could as well, I am achingly aware that each breath is sacred and each hour a gift. I can choose to live small and tight, grounded in fear or joyously open in full receipt of another day.

It was only upon writing and reflection that I could see how our cardiac crash had resulted in a resurrection, which allowed both Charlie and me to begin living our best lives. To heal myself, I began writing not only of what happened, but, more importantly, about how I learned to move through it. How I stopped expecting the worst to happen and began waking up to the wonder in my life. How I am no longer waiting for some day in the future to begin living. How I will never again take for granted the fact that either Charlie or I woke up today.

Making that shift was a long process for me similar to the now-well-researched journey of grief first documented by psychiatrist Elisabeth Kübler-Ross. In her internationally best-selling book *On Death and Dying*, first published in 1969, she outlined the five primary emotions in the stages of grief: anger, denial, bargaining, depression, and acceptance. Although the model became a staple of popular culture and psychology over the last fifty years, it no longer completely explains all the emotions we grapple with in complicated circumstances of possible death after prolonged illness—particularly that final transition from depression to acceptance.

So many of us need, alongside our grief books, the prequel to those stories: a book about breaking. About what happens when some unforeseen event—death, divorce, diagnosis—leaves us shattered. There is not yet a death but we become mired in depression knowing that tragedy is possible, maybe even imminent. Someone we love will leave us, we just don't know when.

We are weighted by our own mortality, certain of this unwelcome knowledge that has entered our lives and, thus, everything has changed. Within this shadow, we cannot celebrate. Under this steady gaze, we cannot look away. We are left then only to bear it. With anxious hearts and already grieving minds, we must learn to live this life with the unwelcome certainty of its end for ourselves and those we love.

At the onset, this knowledge feels unbearable. As if we have shattered and will never again be whole. This shattering, however, also brings new consciousness providing the possibility of transformation. In Japan, there is an ancient art of Kintsugi—repairing broken pottery by filling the cracks with gold. Practitioners of this 400-year-old technique believe these imperfect yet restored pieces are even more beautiful once made whole again. This process of reassembling shards with such a precious metal also makes the original piece an even stronger vessel than before it was broken.

What if we could apply this philosophy to our own lives? Believing that after life-shattering events, we can become not only whole but even stronger than before. The question then becomes this: how do we discover the gold to bind our broken selves?

This book recounts the process of how I found the alchemy for the golden glue that repaired my life. The seven-year journey led me through many more emotions than the five suggested by Dr. Kübler-Ross. In writing and reflecting on life with a rare disease, I felt there were sixteen steps to find my way to whole from Breaking to Being. My journey involved surrendering. It involved conceding there were no answers. It involved accepting radical uncertainty. To do all of this required a daily shift of consciousness. I needed to navigate the labyrinth of wisdom both in the world and in my heart. With insights from both medicine and spirituality, I built the bridge to something I could believe in.

This work helped me discover my own gold epoxy of faith for repairing what shattered my heart. While I may never be grateful for what broke us that day, I will now concede that we became the strongest and most beautiful version of ourselves. No matter what unwanted diagnosis or unfair outcome might someday shatter you, I hope these pages help you rediscover the wonder in your own life, recognize the holy in your every day, and remember—always—that there is no such thing as an ordinary hour.

2

REELING

LEAVING WHO
WE WERE

Forty-two days.

That is how long I had known Charlie before he blurted out over a late-night dinner, "Will you marry me?" There was no champagne and for that matter, no ring, because in the six weeks we had known each other, we had never once discussed marriage.

The moment I saw Charlie, however, it was love at first sight. It was 1985 and I was a twenty-two-year-old seeking adventure in Charlotte. As a recent college graduate from the University of Texas at Austin, my first job offer with an advertising agency was 1,630 miles from my hometown of El Paso. As far away as it was from my home state of Texas, there was also a natural connection to North Carolina. Thirty years before, my parents had met as college students and fallen in love in Charlotte.

Because I had lived my entire life in Texas, my move seven states away had been more difficult than I had expected. For three months, my life consisted of work and late-night TV. Although I had made several acquaintances and gone on a few dates, I did not yet have any real friends in my new city. On a Thursday night, a co-worker invited me to a backyard BBQ. When I arrived at the crowded party alone, I almost immediately went home. Although it was full of young professionals, it seemed as if everyone already knew each other from college. With my hand poised on the wooden white gate leading into the backyard, I had that moment where I just wanted to leave and eat popcorn alone for dinner. It was in this critical moment of determining my exit strategy that I saw him.

Charlie was holding a beer in one hand with his arms crossed as he talked with a guy who was at least four inches shorter. Nearly six feet, four inches tall, Charlie had to bend slightly to hear what his friend was saying. There must have been a great punch line to the story because Charlie stood up straight, tipped his head back and laughed with a full body shake, which also revealed his slight gap-toothed smile. Charlie's sandy-brown hair was cut conservatively around his temples with just a hint of curl on his neckline above a blue-knit shirt. Broad shoulders suggested he might be an athlete but there was no hint of the bravado that sometimes accompanies men accustomed to having their names on the back of their sports jerseys. There was just an ease about Charlie which made me want to draw closer and something inside me whispered: *Yes. Him.*

Pushing through the crowd to stand beside Charlie, I was a full twelve inches shorter. He literally had to look down to see me and in doing so, noticed my empty hands. "Can I get you a beer?" he asked with no Southern accent.

We would talk together for the next two hours, partially penned in by the crowd and partially rooted by a conversation that flowed as easily Charlie's laughter. I learned we each had recently moved and we shared the struggle of navigating our new Southern city. Fresh from New York, Charlie had moved for a job with an investment firm, enticed by the good weather, the lower cost of living, and the promise of no commute. I have no idea what other topics we stretched across those two hours. My only memory was how comfortable I felt with this good-looking guy I hardly knew. In the past three months, all my conversations to make friends had felt so stilted that I had been second-guessing my decision to move so far away from everything I knew in Texas. That night talking to Charlie was the very first time I felt at home.

It was after midnight when I finally left the party. Driving back to my apartment, there was a full smile stretched across my face as I sang along with the car radio on full volume. When I put the key into the metal door of my apartment, I could hear my landline ringing. Hurrying in to answer, I picked up the phone and heard the voice of one of my best friends from El Paso, "How's it going in Charlotte?"

"Great! I met the guy I am going to marry," I said in a wild hope before realizing I had not given Charlie my phone number.

So while he couldn't call me, I knew where to find Charlie because he had told me he worked out at the YMCA every day after work. Within twenty-four hours, I had joined that gym but it would take two weeks of fitness classes before I would see Charlie Izard again. Sitting in my car wearing a grungy T-shirt after a particularly difficult aerobics class, I spotted him crossing the parking lot. Rolling down my window, I called out and Charlie turned my way. It took him a minute to recognize me with my brown bangs plastered with sweat to my forehead.

"Hey!" he said breaking into that grin I already had fallen in love with. We made small talk for a moment, and then, he fumbled before getting his words out.

"You wouldn't want to have a beer with me would you?" he asked.

It felt like I had been waiting my whole life for that question. That began our six-week romance where Charlie cooked for me from his mother's recipes or he bought dinner in nice restaurants. It was on that forty-second day that I had finally invited him to my apartment even though I was a terrible cook. Trout amandine was a disastrous choice for a novice chef, but the wine was flowing. Maybe it was the combination of too little food and too much drink that caused Charlie to blurt out that very unplanned and unexpected, "Will you marry me?"

I wanted to leap across the across the couch and say *YES* with all my heart but at the same time, I couldn't trust that it wasn't merely the wine talking. At my core, I truly couldn't believe that this amazing guy I had fallen for actually loved me in return.

"I don't think you meant to say that," I told him. "So, if in thirty minutes you can even remember the question, I will give you an answer."

Charlie smiled. We drank a little more wine. I tried not to show how desperately I wanted him to remember the question. He did and within the year, we said, "I Do."

It was a risky love for both of us. We were each betting a lifetime on a perfect stranger. There was so much we didn't know about each other and in many ways we were a mismatch. Charlie was exactly a foot taller and one hundred pounds heavier that I was. He was accustomed to northern snow and I was at home in the western desert. He balanced his checkbook to the exact penny and I opened my monthly statements only to verify that I had not bounced a check.

But over the course or those forty-two dinners, we had already agreed on many of life's pressing issues in an increasing order of seriousness.

Italian, yes. Sushi, no.

Dogs, yes. Cats, no.

Football, yes. Baseball, no.

A promise must be kept.

Character counts.

Trust requires no exceptions.

Children, yes. Lots of them.

We moved quickly from newlyweds to homeowners, to dog owners, to parents. Our first daughter, Lauren, was born in January 1989, three days before I turned twenty-six. Seventeen months later, Kailey came into the world, and the surprise ending to our family was twin girls, Maddie and Emma born in 1994. Coincidentally, our first home was just around the corner from where my parents had met while my mom was a student at Queens College and my dad attended Davidson College.

Growing up, my hope had always been to build a family life overflowing with kids, dogs, and laughter. When we first met, I had no idea that was exactly how Charlie was raised by his parents, Bob and Jean. Charlie was the middle of five children born in six years. Bobby, Nancy, Charlie, Elizabeth, David. His childhood home was a gray clapboard colonial perched on a slight hill in the quiet suburban community of Rye, New York—just outside the city. It was always filled not only with the Izard children and dogs but the neighborhood kids and dogs as well. On a typical Saturday morning, his mom would whip up waffles for her five children, several neighborhood boys, her two dachshunds, and the next door neighbor's basset hound, Falstaff. Every human knew to wait patiently because in Jean's kitchen, the dogs were always served first.

We developed a similar Saturday ritual except that Charlie didn't believe in feeding our two corgis, Ellie and Emmitt, "people" food. Lauren, Kailey, Emma, and Maddie would perch on the kitchen-counter stools watching their dad dazzle them with breakfast. Charlie would pour the batter into three overlapping circles to make "Mickey Mouse" pancakes dripping in butter and syrup. Afterwards, the girls would wrestle with their dad climbing on him like a giggly pack of puppies. While we didn't have four sons, Charlie taught our four daughters all of life's essential skills like catching a football and sinking a three-point basketball shot.

Charlie loved any outdoor sport and the more adrenalin producing the better. In fact, he chose pursuits precisely because they posed an element of danger. He didn't have a death wish, he simply loved testing his body. After years of middle school, high school, and college sports, Charlie missed the punishing workouts and high-level competition. Along with the camaraderie among teammates, Charlie craved those moments when coaches asked for the impossible and he pushed past exhaustion to deliver even more reps than required.

So it was not really surprising when in his late forties, Charlie first mentioned wanting to attempt heli-skiing. This version of hitting the slopes first began in the 1950s in Alaska and Europe to access high peaks without ski lifts. Charlie's cousin, also named Charlie, was planning a boys' trip to the Canadian Selkirk Mountains. Talking about the details of the adventure, my Charlie was as excited as an eight-year-old boy on Christmas morning.

"We would stay in a lodge that is only accessible by helicopter!" Charlie told me. "Every day they take us to the top of different peaks and we ski untouched powder!"

To me, it sounded like a week of terror, but to Charlie, it promised to be a week of thrills. I knew Charlie really wasn't asking my permission, he just wanted my blessing.

"You have to call once a day, every day to let me know you are safe," I told him.

"I am a good skier, Kathy," he told me. "Nothing is going to happen."

I never really worried Charlie might actually die heli-skiing because he was just too healthy and too athletic. While I had no desire to attempt this sport, I understood why Charlie found it so exhilarating. Even after his third season, Charlie had not tired of the rush and trained all year for this one-week test of his physical limits. The other fifty-one weeks, Charlie wore a gray suit to sit at a desk in a glass office tower with his heart rate rising and falling by the whims of the stock market. But this annual trek to the Canadian Rockies had become the closest Charlie came to his memories of being an All-American lacrosse player pushing his body in a championship game. After he came home, Charlie's joy would continue in a monthlong happiness hangover.

While he was in the Canadian mountains, his promised daily phone calls were always filled with the most exuberant, boyish excitement.

"This was the best day ever!" he would yell through the static on the satellite phone. "It's really like being on top of the world."

I could picture Charlie's grin stretching beneath his eyes with a tan line from his ski goggles making him resemble a cheery racoon.

"On top of those mountains, I feel like the luckiest guy alive," Charlie said.

When the doctor who saved Charlie's life came into our cramped ICU quarters, we realized Charlie truly was one of the luckiest guys alive. Calm and confident, Dr. Omar Ali entered our cramped surgical recovery room and stood at the end of Charlie's bed seemingly as surprised to be there as we were. With his cap removed, his thick black hair was unleashed from an average afternoon saving a life. Well over six feet tall, Dr. Ali towered over me and he had a slight five-o'clock shadow on his upper lip and chin. As he reached for my hand to introduce himself, I felt a sense of safety about this doctor that radiated beyond the fact that he had just performed a miracle on my soul mate.

"I have only seen one of these," Dr. Ali said shaking his head slightly in disbelief as he spoke. "I may never see another one again."

I still didn't understand what *it* was. This thing that had just shattered our lives.

"Charlie, what happened to you is called SCAD: Spontaneous Coronary Artery Dissection," Dr. Ali said. "Very rare. Usually only happens to women after an extreme stress like childbirth."

Charlie and I stared back at the doctor, one of us too drugged and one of us too shocked to even understand what questions we should be asking.

"You are a very lucky guy," Dr. Ali said. "Your LAD (left anterior descending artery) is the most important artery in the front of your heart. It carries fresh blood and provides the oxygen your heart needs to pump properly. If your LAD is blocked, your heart will suddenly stop. When you arrived, your LAD was already completely closed," Dr. Ali paused to see if we were understanding this instant cardiac education we were receiving.

"The gold standard for intervention is within one hour. When a patient's LAD is obstructed for longer than sixty minutes, the mortality rate starts to increase significantly. Your sixty minutes had already started at the urgent care. We didn't have a lot of time," Dr. Ali explained.

The miracle was slowly sinking in to both of us just how fortunate we were that Charlie arrived at this cardiac catherization lab in less than an hour.

"Typically, a blockage is caused by plaque but your arteries, they are pristine, really pristine," Dr. Ali marveled. "Your blockage was caused by something really rare—it spontaneously dissected."

I tried to keep up but I felt like I needed to consult a medical encyclopedia with some photos for clarification. Dr. Ali was already moving on guiding us to the final chapter.

"Some call that particular artery the *widow-maker*, because when it is blocked without immediate intervention, the survival rates can be very low." Dr. Ali paused. "As rare as SCAD is, the survival rate for women is much higher than for men. Unfortunately for males, it is a diagnosis usually only discovered after an autopsy."

Autopsy. That word stopped me cold. What Dr. Ali was trying to say is that Charlie should be dead, but somehow, against all odds, he was alive.

I knew we should be asking more questions, yet I didn't even know where to begin.

"But why couldn't his cardiologist in Charlotte see this?" I asked. "Charlie had arm pain and chest pain—why did that doctor tell him it was just stress?"

"That is the most unusual part about SCAD—you cannot see it before it happens," said Dr. Ali shaking his head. "Because the dissection occurs within the artery itself, we cannot see it until after it happens. As of now, there is no test we can use to predict or prevent it in patients with SCAD."

"But it won't happen again?" I interrupted. "Now that he has these two stents to keep his artery open, it can't happen again, right?"

Dr. Ali shifted his gaze to Charlie and then back to me, not quite meeting my eyes when he answered, "We can't really say. There are so few patients with SCAD that I am afraid there is very little research to predict."

Through the fog of pain medicine, Charlie wasn't talking so I wasn't sure what he was comprehending. Was he hearing what I was hearing? That this horrible, blindsiding event may not be over? That it could actually happen again? At any time with no warning?

Understanding my escalating panic, Dr. Ali tried to reassure me, "What happened today is what we call a 'black swan event.' It hardly ever happens." He paused as we stood on either side of the hospital bed with Charlie between us. "Charlie, is very lucky to be here."

Over the next few hours, we would begin to realize just how lucky Charlie was. Any number of things could have gone differently. If Charlie had taken a nap. If the urgent care had not called an ambulance. If Charlie had not been in peak physical condition. If the cardiac lab had already been closed for the day.

Any one of those steps could have gone differently in the sixty minutes between Charlie collapsing on the hotel room bed and the wild ambulance ride that delivered him to Dr. Ali's safe, skilled hands. Everything had miraculously lined up so that Charlie was still holding my hand.

Everything worked just perfectly so that I was making phone calls to find hotel rooms near the hospital instead of notifying our next of kin. I knew it was more than possible that I could have ended this day with the unimaginable task of trying to find a funeral home seven states away from our home.

While he remembered he was going to take a nap, Charlie was completely unaware of all that had transpired in the past few hours. The rental car abandoned at the urgent care. The ambulance ride to an unknown hospital. The phone calls on a phone borrowed from a nurse to begin spreading the news.

Dad, yes, your Dad had a heart attack.

I still don't fully know how each of the girls made it there. I have no idea what trains, planes, or automobiles were arranged in a series of frantic calls so that all of our daughters arrived to be with us. We would discover that the ambulance had taken us almost thirty minutes from the urgent care near our hotel to Lowell General Hospital in Lowell, Massachusetts. It had been only twelve hours since that seemingly benign turkey-sandwich lunch in a New England café and yet in that time, our world had shifted.

It was midnight on the longest day I had ever known and all of us were gathered together. Charlie had been moved to a cardiac ICU room, and we stood around him shoulder to shoulder holding hands in what felt like a particularly sacred circle of six.

"Charlie's Angels," Charlie said smiling up at all of us.

Charlie was weak and so his words were whispered but we all understood the pun. It was an old family joke that started one Christmas when the girls were dressed in wings and halos for the church Christmas pageant.

It was still so difficult for all of us to believe.

Charlie had a heart attack.

My heli-skiing husband, who exercised fiendishly and still had the physique of a college athlete, almost died today. It made no sense. I had no words to explain to my daughters how this happened, yet they all wanted me to give them some comfort or some assurance. Their tear-stained faces looked back at me for answers but there weren't any.

Maddie had given Charlie a navy-blue mug one Christmas. It was oversized with a hefty handle and it had a Superman logo in steel gray on one side and a graphic of the flying Clark Kent on the other. In the image, Superman appears to crash through the side of the mug—arms outstretched, red cape billowing behind him—with a determined look of imagined victory. Most mornings, Charlie sipped his coffee out of this mug as he read the morning paper. To see another man drink from that same cup might have seemed silly. But to the five of us who loved Charlie, it really wasn't a joke.

We always believed he was Superman. We always believed he could achieve superhuman tasks. And until today, we always believed that their dad and my Goose, might even be immortal.

I have thought a lot about that hour before it all happened, eating unremarkable sandwiches in the café, discussing weather and school drama, blissfully unaware that cardiac arteries can, for no known reason, spontaneously split. I think now how it was before we knew. Before all of us—me, Charlie, and our daughters, Lauren, Kailey, Emma, and Maddie—received a warp-speed, medical trauma education with a specialization in rare cardiac anomalies.

Poet David Whyte talks about doors you don't want to go through. *The Cancer Door. The Divorce Door. The Losing a Child Door.* When we are confronted with the eventual agonies of life, untimely deaths, and unwanted diagnosis, we are left reeling in front of difficult doors we do not want to pass through. We learn, however, that we don't get a choice. When we are standing on the threshold of pain and loss, we are unexpectedly shoved through those doorways and always in shock. Our family had just been pushed through doors we never imagined walking through. *The Heart Attack Door. The SCAD Door. The Rare Disease Door.* When that happened, the *Normal Living Door* slammed firmly behind us.

Dr. Rachel Naomi Remen is clinical professor of Family and Community Medicine at UCSF School of Medicine and the founder and director of the Institute for the Study of Health and Illness at Wright State University Boonshoft School of Medicine in Dayton, Ohio. As a physician, she pioneered the idea integrating faith and healing. Her curriculum "The Healer's Art" is now taught yearly in more than half of American medical schools and in medical schools in seven countries around the world. Dr. Remen writes:

> Most people try to hold onto the thing that is no longer part of their lives and they stop themselves in their lives in that way. I have come to see loss as a stage in a process. It's not the bottom line. It's not the end of the story. What happens next is very, very important.

In that ICU ward in the Lowell General Hospital, it was impossible to see what might happen next. Standing in that unwanted SCAD doorway, I could not begin to fathom how we might begin to cope. Charlie and I both wanted desperately to go back to the way we were before, to the life we had before, but we had already crossed over that threshold. Eventually, we would understand that unexpected passage would mark the beginning of our transformation.

3

COPING

MEDICAL EMERGENCIES LEAD
TO SPIRITUAL EMERGENCIES

When loss forces us over the threshold to unexpected places, we have to begin new ways of coping and, typically, this begins with support from others. With a death, there begins a grieving process with no timeline for recovery. With a new diagnosis, friends and acquaintances with any related condition will offer the phone numbers for their doctors or information about their support groups. With a rare disease, however, there is often no advice that friends can give and no specialist's name to pass along. Although we had asked Dr. Ali for a SCAD support group or another patient we might contact, he had shaken his head. "I am sorry, I don't know of any."

With no one we knew dealing with such a rare cardiac disease, we were left fumbling on our own. While Charlie went back to work trying to pretend nothing ever happened or would ever happen again, I stewed at home under an insidious fog that seemed impossible to lift. I had a nervous energy coursing through my body at all times—as if I was a fireman waiting for a fire. Every time my phone buzzed, I jumped. Was it Charlie? Was he in an ambulance? Did I need to meet him at the hospital?

I paced our kitchen and alternated between eating chocolate chips and potato chips hoping the cacao and salt might soothe anxiety running through my veins. As if in filling my body, I could cure Charlie's. Hour after hour on my laptop, I disappeared down a medical research rabbit hole trying to find anything I could about "Spontaneous Coronary Artery Dissection." I needed to feel like I had plan of action and searching the Internet gave me hope that I could Google our way out of our crisis. On one deep-dive day on a website, I discovered that typing in "SCAD" brought me to a link for an online chat group called WomenHeart.

Scanning the page of hundreds of posts, I realized that there were about seventy female members who regularly traded information about cardiac issues that were specific to SCAD. As small a group as that was, it made me feel less alone. Scrolling through the posts, it seemed Katherine Leon managed the forum, actively providing encouragement and information. In her online photo, Katherine smiled warmly from my laptop screen. With auburn hair and fair skin, she was a youngish forty-eight-year-old, who looked like we could become friends over a steaming cup of tea. To begin our virtual friendship, I typed:

> *Katherine,*
> *I think my very healthy husband, Charlie, may have SCAD. He had*
> *a heart attack and they put in two stents. We don't have a lot more*
> *information but I found your online group and hoping you can provide*
> *some answers.*
> *Kathy*

Katherine responded right away just as she had been doing for several years when newly diagnosed patients from all over the world searched online for SCAD. Ten years before, Katherine had never heard of this rare disease either. In 2003, she was home nursing her newborn baby boy when she began having chest pain, arm numbness, and shortness of breath.

At her local emergency room, Katherine's complaints were dismissed. The hospital staff told her she was too young and too healthy to have a heart attack. A week later, Katherine returned to the same hospital and was finally diagnosed with a 90% blockage of her left main artery. After an emergency double bypass surgery, Katherine woke up with the same diagnosis as Charlie—Spontaneous Coronary Artery Dissection.

Katherine had asked her cardiologist for information about SCAD, but like us, she learned there wasn't any. Although she had no medical background, Katherine dove into SCAD reading what little she could find online before turning to social media to find other women struggling with this same rare disease. Eventually, she created a SCAD group on the WomenHeart forum and through that volunteer work, Katherine applied to attend a training in Rochester, Minnesota, at the famed Mayo Clinic.

It was the first time Katherine had been on a plane since her heart attack and she was terrified. But she knew she would have the opportunity to meet many world-class experts, including Dr. Sharonne Hayes a respected Mayo cardiologist. Katherine hoped that perhaps a female doctor might be intrigued by a mystery condition that primarily plagued women. After one of Dr. Hayes's presentations at the WomenHeart training, Katherine approached the cardiologist to ask her questions.

"Why isn't anyone conducting research on SCAD?" Katherine asked.

"There are not enough patients to conduct a study," Dr. Hayes replied.

"Well, I know at least seventy," Katherine told her.

"How do you know seventy SCAD patients?" Dr. Hayes asked.

"I met them online!" Katherine answered.

Thus began the first medical research study in the world started through social media. After recounting this story to me on our call, Katherine provided Dr. Hayes's direct contact information. If there was only one doctor in the United States studying SCAD, I wanted Charlie to see her. Making an appointment at Mayo was easier than I expected but we still had to wait eight weeks for a June opening on Dr. Hayes's schedule. As impatient as I was, we had to live in the tension of the unknown, waiting to see if there was a cardiologist who could give us hope.

While we waited for our appointment at the Mayo Clinic, I searched for ways to deal with my unrelenting anxiety about our situation. Friends who practiced yoga suggested it might help me cope with our new reality.

Notice your breath, the instructor told me in my first hot-yoga class. I tried to do as she said. To think about my own breathing. My own oxygen level. Flight attendants always say when you are on a plane, "Apply your own before helping your child or those around you."

But I found it difficult those days to think about anyone other than Charlie.

Was his chest rising and falling right now? Where was he?

Every night it seemed I spent more and more time obsessively watching his chest move up and down. Wide awake, my eyes would focus on the brief rise and fall of his chest. If I wasn't sure, I would sit up, squinting and searching for movement by the faint light of our digital clock. This slight movement was my only clue that Charlie's heart was still beating safely. The doctor said there would be no warning. What if he died while I slept? What if I woke to a cold, unmoving Charlie?

That was the thought that kept returning in the night making it impossible to sleep. Before we went to bed, Charlie and I always kissed good night no matter what had happened in the day. This was sage advice from his parents who were married over fifty years. Even if we had been in a huge fight, Charlie's parents told us to remember why we loved each other before going to sleep no matter how mad we still were. We would always kiss good night, and then find our respective sleeping positions curled back to back. I would slide my foot down Charlie's calf to rest my arch along the curve of his leg.

This I how I generally woke each morning, my right foot stretching toward the warmth of Charlie's smooth, muscled calf. And this is what terrified me. What if one morning, that stretch for warmth was instead cold? What if Charlie somehow died in his sleep while I slumbered unknowingly next to him? What if I had not been awake in the night to notice and rush him to a hospital? What then? What was my first step as a widow?

The yoga instructor repeated, *Cobra Pose,* and I realized I had been left worrying about Charlie in Downward Dog while the class had moved on. I felt like that a lot lately. Like Charlie and I were in one place and the world had moved on. Everyone was consumed with busyness and moving faster. We were stuck in the moment-by-moment tick of every single heartbeat like watching grains of sand falling in an hourglass—except we were not really watching the sand.

We were waiting for that unpredictable, inexplicable moment when the glass would spontaneously shatter and the sand would explode into the air.

Fifteen years before, I experienced this same feeling of being out of sync with the world when my dad was being treated for Acute Myeloid Leukemia at Houston's MD Anderson Cancer Treatment Center. Every time I flew to Texas to spend several days with Dad in his small glass treatment room, it seemed time stopped on that cancer campus. Everyone living in that oncology world had a different sense of time than everyone outside of it. We all knew why we were there. We all knew the urgency of each day. Once I returned to my life in Charlotte, the precariousness of life so preciously pulsing at my father's bedside would fade once I returned to the carpools and soccer schedules of raising our four young daughters.

With Charlie's heart issues, the suspension of time felt the same but the urgency never left us. There wasn't a place we were living in hope of an experimental cure, and then, a place we went to recover. We weren't being treated and we weren't fighting this disease. We were simply coping the best we could. And waiting. Waiting to see if Charlie's heart would stop or an artery would split again. Waiting to see the one specialist, Dr. Sharonne Hayes, who might be able to give us some answers.

In my hot-yoga class, the man next to me was dripping an insane amount of bodily fluids onto the floor next me. It had been two months since Charlie had broken such a sweat. Now, it was impossible for Charlie to work up a bead of perspiration on his plodding, four-mile walks—his only allowable exercise. No running. No racing his heart. Nothing that would cause the blood to surge through his heart and possibly give way to another dissected artery.

Checking my watch through my Warrior arm position, I saw there were twenty-seven minutes left in the class—a really long time for something that wasn't helping my anxiety. I rolled up my mat and quietly left class long before it was over. It felt liberating to have a choice in something when everything else in our life felt so out of control.

That night at dinner, I decided we needed to talk about it. Two months after our cardiac emergency, we had stopped discussing Charlie's health. Maybe we thought if we didn't talk about it, it would not happen again. It would just go away. Like when you wake up in a sweaty panic from a vivid nightmare but later that day, you can't even remember what had startled you awake.

We were sitting side by side on the stools at the kitchen counter. When all the girls were at home, we used to eat dinner in our kitchen at

6:30 at the large round table with six, blue, wooden chairs. But now that the girls were in school or working, Charlie and I had moved our meals to the counter. It felt less like we were waiting for four dinner guests to arrive when we were seated at the counter.

"You still think about it?" I asked breaking our silence. Maybe I was the only one dwelling on death. Maybe he had found a way to stop thinking about heart attacks and splitting arteries all the time.

Charlie didn't even look up from his grilled chicken and green beans when he answered. He just stared at his fork as he said, "Only every minute of every day."

While Charlie had survived his medical emergency, each day that passed in our new normal, I felt like my life was in a serious spiritual emergency. I needed something to help me feel safe and grounded in these new days where each hour, each minute I worried about Charlie. There were no answers to be found on the Internet. There was no food that could fill my aching soul. There was no yoga pose that could make me feel more peaceful.

Until this moment, I had always been able to solve almost any problem through cleverness, stubbornness, or plain persistence. But SCAD presented a diagnosis with no pill, no protocol, and no prognosis. For the first time in my life, I was facing an unsolvable problem.

I felt like the only person I could talk to about all this was my therapist, Tammie. I was grateful I had a trusted professional to call because until I was in my forties, I never thought I needed one. I had always just dealt with difficult things When I was six years old, my mother was hospitalized for the first of several episodes that doctors finally determined was a bipolar disorder. I believed all those years growing up enduring my mom cycling through mania and depression had not really affected me.

By the time I was twenty-two, Mom was finally prescribed the right medicine, which rebalanced her brilliant brain. She returned to being the enormously talented woman that she had always been, serving on our church council and leading the choir. My entire family just never mentioned the fact that Mom had missed most of our childhood. It was as if we had shaken an Etch A Sketch to erase all the unpleasant memories.

But raising four daughters made me realize that there were cracks beginning to appear in my very carefully constructed life. I wanted to be the mom with all the answers, but I had none because my own childhood had been so full of questions. I felt completely unprepared to raise my girls because I had a fuzzy memory of my own upbringing. For the past few years, I had been unpacking all that I had not wanted to remember and processing it with Tammie. It felt like she was the only person who could help me navigate our new radical uncertainty.

Just like there had been no warning for my mother's unpredictable mood swings there would be no warning for Charlie's impending cardiac crash. I craved certainty and there was no certainty with SCAD.

"This idea that Charlie's cardiac arteries might split at any time? How do I live with that?" I asked Tammie.

She handed me the tissue box. I had been through a lot of Kleenex in her office. It was the one place I felt safe to cry. In front of friends and family, I tried to be the eternal optimist.

Yes, it's true Charlie had a heart attack but we are so lucky he is alive!

It was a miracle!

We are going to live every moment of every day!

Except we weren't. I was living every day as if Charlie had maybe sixty seconds left before he expired.

"It's the not knowing," I told Tammie. "If he had cancer we could feel like we were fighting it. Or at least like we have a fighting chance. There's nothing to fight. There's no way to plan."

"And you like a plan?"

"I love a plan. A plan I can execute. A plan I can check off," I said.

"And this all feels out of your control."

"Exactly!" I said.

Tammie pulled a book off her shelf and handed me a copy of Richard Rohr's *Falling Upward: A Spirituality for the Two Halves of Life.* "Have you read this?"

I shook my head. Although I loved reading, I used books as an escape. A great mystery novel or some quirky fiction had always been a wonderful way to distract myself. My bookshelves were full of great reads, but during the past few months I could not find any titles that delivered distraction. With every book I opened, I became restless after only a few pages because the subject was not what I needed. I wanted to find an author who had answers about living with extreme uncertainty.

"You might like Rohr's writing," Tammie suggested. "His book is all about struggle and what that might mean."

That night, I started reading and couldn't stop. With chapter titles like "Necessary Suffering," the book was exactly the master class I needed. Rohr writes:

It is not that suffering or failure might happen, or that it will only hap-pen to you if you are bad (which is what religious people often think), or that it will happen to the unfortunate, or to a few in other places, or that you can somehow by cleverness or righteousness avoid it. No, it will happen, and to you! Losing, failing, falling, sin, and the suffering that comes from those experiences—all of this is a necessary and even good part of the human journey.

That was a revelation. I did believe I could avoid suffering. I did believe that somehow if I was clever and resourceful enough I could direct my life away from any unexpected pain—like my dad dying from

leukemia or my mom suffering with a bipolar diagnosis. Rohr insists
that struggle is inevitable and, actually, necessary to grow in our human
experience. He contends that as long as we spend our lives distracted by
human pursuits (success or wealth accumulation) we will never attend to
the more crucial spiritual pursuits. It is usually only after some life crisis
like an illness or tragedy, that we seek the strength of a higher power.

In my own life, my belief system was really just more of scaffolding
built around an attitude of gratitude. There was nothing behind the
façade. While I had a reverence for God, I held no true trust in a higher
power. I did not have a faith strong enough for this relentless daily fear.
SCAD had truly brought me to my knees with no idea how I was going
to rise up, much less remain standing.

Reading *Falling Upward* started a whole new section of my home
library. I read every other book by Rohr, and then other modern spiritual teachers like Barbara Brown Taylor, Sue Monk Kidd, and Frederick
Buechner. My favorite lighthearted beach reads by well-known novelists
began to share space on my shelves with famous faith writers. I no longer
wanted to be distracted when I read—I wanted to be fed.

The more I read, the more I understood how pain is not optional.
It is inevitable. James Baldwin wrote, "*You think your pain and your heart-
break are unprecedented in the history of the world, but then you read. It was
books that taught me that the things that tormented me the most were the very
things that connected me with all the people who were alive, or who had ever
been alive.*"

My new reading not only connected me to so many authors, it prompted
me to write. Initially, I composed my thoughts in journals, and then I
began formalizing my words on my laptop. My feelings and memories
were a like a ball of yarn in the pit of my stomach where the more I

unspooled words onto the page, the lighter I felt. Reading, writing, and reflecting became the lifeboat sent to rescue my drifting life.

So much of what I thought I knew to be true about religion was a gospel for the good news.

Ask and you shall receive.

God helps those who help themselves.

God will provide.

I didn't know until I began reading that this is called "prosperity theology," which promises that financial blessing and physical well-being are always the will of God. It assumes there is a contract between humans and God: if you have unwavering faith, God will deliver only good things.

But what about when faith and medical science collide? What about when there is no hope and there is a 100% chance of fatality? What if no medical miracles are possible? What then? This gospel of good news cannot always be true. What about believing even in the bad news? A dogma for despair? A hymn for the hopeless?

Often it takes the collision with the unexpected to make someone question prosperity theology. In *An Altar in the World: A Geography of Faith*, professor and former Episcopal priest, Barbara Brown Taylor writes:

> *Deep suffering makes theologians of us all. The questions people ask about God in Sunday school rarely compare to the questions we ask while we are in the hospital.*

I was just beginning to understand what those questions might be and Barbara Brown Taylor's writing held many answers for me. In *Learning to Walk in the Dark*, Taylor describes a new understanding of faith that began to resonate with me.

I have learned things in the dark that I could never have learned in the light, things that have saved my life over and over again, so that there is really only one logical conclusion. I need darkness as much as I need light.

I had spent much of my life in the light. When Charlie and I crossed the SCAD threshold however, we entered what felt like a dim world. I couldn't yet see in that dark. Some mornings our world felt so bleak I could only pull the covers more tightly over my head. It takes peeking out from under the comforter to witness any kind of light. When I finally did, just as Barbara Brown Taylor suggested, I realized there was so much to learn in the dark that I had never pondered in the light.

4

FALLING

WHEN BAD NEWS BECOMES
WORSE NEWS

In navigating a new diagnosis, there are often levels of understanding that we must pass through. There is the initial shock of a new disease. The first time we are told that our bodies might be failing us in ways that could lead to complications if not addressed through surgery or treatment. It might be our general practitioner, an emergency room doctor, or, as in Charlie's case, a surgeon, who delivers the initial bad news. The scan that is suspicious. The blood level that is elevated. The lump that needs a biopsy. As we get deeper into a medical maze, it is often a specialist that delivers the more devasting news and it feels as if we have fallen into a pit that has no escape.

In heli-skiing this type of pit is called a *tree well*. I had never heard of such a danger until Charlie took up this sport six years before his heart attack. For four days a year, he would willingly jump out of a helicopter at the top of 10,000-foot peaks and race to the bottom. He would come home from these epic adventures with enough adrenalin to last until the next year when he would do it all over again. As dangerous as that sounds, I never worried much about Charlie then because he was such a good athlete. I thought his greatest risk was a broken bone. Little did I know that the only truly potentially fatal hazards were these tree wells.

While not particularly dangerous on groomed slopes, backcountry skiers and heli-skiers learn to be wary. At high elevations, the branches of pine trees become covered in thick snow. The boughs catch the majority of snowflakes, which means at the base, the snow accumulates lightly; there is no solid base around the trunks. These areas in the forests are perilous because they cannot bear a person's weight. If a skier skids too close to one of these hidden, lightly packed tree wells, he will immediately fall into a cavern disappearing from the surface. Once someone falls into a tree well, suffocation only takes minutes. Rescue must happen swiftly if the trapped skier is to survive.

After Charlie's heart attack, I felt as if we had fallen into a tree well, but I still believed someone was coming rescue us. All my hopes were pinned on Dr. Sharonne Hayes at Mayo Clinic to be our savior. We had no idea we could be any more scared than we already were. We did not know it was possible to fall any further—and keep falling. We had not contemplated that there was no one coming to dig us out.

When we landed after a two-hour-and-forty-five-minute flight to Minneapolis, it was still a ninety-minute drive across Minnesota farmlands to reach Rochester, home of the primary Mayo Clinic. With his cardiac dissection confirmed by researchers who reviewed his records, Charlie was in fact, a "SCAD survivor." There were now over 400 patients in the Mayo Clinic SCAD study started by Katherine Leon's online support group. When the study began, it was predominantly female; Charlie became only the tenth male the Mayo team had accepted into their research.

Mayo Clinic is, quite literally, the entire town of Rochester. One-third of the city's population, over 34,000 people, are employed by this huge center, which is a medical destination for patients from around the world who fly here, like us, for hope. Charlie had downloaded the Mayo app before we arrived and all of his appointments for consultations were magically tracked on his phone. *Lab work. EKG. PET scan.*

PET scan? Charlie had a cardiac problem, why would they scan his whole body with this high-level test? Over the next hour and a half, Dr. Hayes explained this and much more as she went over all the results. Her manicured hands gestured elegantly and easily to Charlie's charts and complicated cardiac history.

"Arteries have an inner lining," she explained, reminding us what Dr. Ali told us months ago. "These linings are actually what split and dissect causing the artery to collapse."

Dr. Hayes pointed to the monitor in her office highlighting the same image of Charlie's heart we had seen before. In this picture, his heart appeared light gray with arteries twisting like tiny, steel-gray snakes except one which was barely a wisp on the screen. Pointing to this weak spot, Dr. Hayes informed us that this was the cause of Charlie's heart attack February 22, 2013.

Since neither of us had a professional medical background, staring at these complicated gray and white lines was confusing. As she spoke, Dr. Hayes confidently gestured as if everything we were seeing on the screen was as crystal clear to us as it was to her. Then, Dr. Hayes delivered the news that became our deepest tree-well moment.

"Through our research, we have realized that while SCAD patients most often present with cardiac issues, other arteries in the body can dissect as well," Dr. Hayes said.

It took us a minute to fully understand that one. Keeping her face calm, Dr. Hayes waited patiently as we processed her statement, letting the information slowly sink in.

"Wait, you mean this can happen anywhere in my body, not just my heart?" Charlie clarified.

"Yes," Dr. Hayes repeated. "While SCAD is seen most often in the cardiac world, our research has discovered that dissections can actually happen in any artery in the body. Carotid arteries, femoral arteries, anywhere. SCAD patients have an all-over body weakness. It is not just a problem with arteries in the heart."

Charlie looked as if Dr. Hayes had just punched him in the face.

"As you know, we have hundreds in our study now, but Charlie, you are one of only ten men— very rare in an already rare disease," Dr. Hayes confirmed. "We have found that when we do full-body PET scans, we generally find other dissections. In your case, Charlie, we did find you had another dissection in your left iliac artery."

We looked up at another gray picture of Charlie's pelvis and this one had a much thicker light-gray line twisting through it. Sure enough, on the screen, it looked as if a tree trunk that started out as one, became two and then reunited as one again. Charlie shook his head in disbelief.

"When did that happen?" he asked.

"We can't be sure," Dr. Hayes answered. "Maybe months ago or maybe years ago."

Charlie paused staring at the screen and then, back to the bearer of bad news.

"You mean that any artery, at any time, and anywhere in my body can just split—for no reason and with no warning?" Charlie asked.

Dr. Hayes nodded.

"And we can't know when it will happen and there is nothing I can do about it?"

"Well, yes, but there are some things you can do to minimize your risks," Dr. Hayes said trying to ease his panic. "We don't advise running, skiing, or playing tennis because that might cause the blood to push too quickly through your arteries. Don't lift anything over ten to twenty pounds. Don't let your heart rate rise above 130."

I watched Charlie, former adrenalin junkie, absorb this devastating information. I know we both had held out hope that this visit would take us back to normal. That Dr. Hayes would tell us that all the danger was behind us and that Charlie could resume his high-activity, heli-skiing days. But Dr. Hayes was telling us the exact opposite.

"Research has shown that once SCAD happens, a patient has a higher risk of reoccurrence the next three years after an event," she added.

This was new news as well.

Charlie was in even more danger now in the next three years? I really was hoping the bad news was behind us. Until that moment, I know we both believed all this careful living was temporary. Like resting after surgery but eventually regaining full function—full life. We were ready to go back to our full, normal life.

"For the next three years, you should always try to be within one hour of a cardiac catherization lab," Dr. Hayes advised.

"One hour from a hospital?" I asked unsure why that mattered.

"There is a sixty-minute window which is crucial if your arteries are blocked again," Dr. Hayes explained. "The outcomes are much better for patients who get to a hospital within one hour of a cardiac arrest."

Or else they die. That is what she meant. Get to a hospital within one hour *or you die.* We all knew what Dr. Hayes meant she was just too kind to say it.

We left Dr. Hayes's office in complete shock. As we had hoped, we had just learned much more about SCAD. Most of it, however, was news I would really rather not know. Wandering to an outdoor café table, we dutifully ordered lunch from the waitress who seemed very comfortable dealing with shell-shocked patients.

What could I say to Charlie? *It was going to be ok?* I was the optimist of the two of us. I always had a positive outlook. Charlie was the always cautious one. I jokingly called him "Eeyore" because he was always taking the glass-half-empty approach. I was the glass-half-full girl, but now I felt nothing but raw fear. We were not going to wake up from this bad dream and find a new or better day. Reaching across the black iron table, I touched Charlie's hand and he instinctively wrapped my fingers in his without turning his head to meet my eyes.

I always felt I could curl into Charlie's embrace, tucked under his arm like a protective angel wing and now, I wanted to be able to comfort Charlie under my own wing. Some kind of divine shield or magical cape that could keep all of this bad news and bad arteries at bay. His whole life, Charlie had meticulously taken care of his body assuming he was in control of his health and thus, in charge of his destiny. That same body was now failing him, and there was nothing we could do to protect or save him. We just had to wait and see what happened.

We had ordered lunch but really, had not been able to speak. Charlie finally turned from staring at all the busy pedestrians on the plaza to gaze directly at me. I am sure anyone passing us that day might have thought we were absorbing bad news about a parent. Someone else in this picture had to be the recipient of a medical death sentence—not the handsome, seemingly healthy-looking man. We had walked into Dr. Hayes's office full of hope like a buoyant balloon bouquet just bobbing and waiting to be released in celebration. But there had been an instant and dramatic pop of expectation that exploded all our optimism of a return to normal living.

"I feel . . ." he began but stopped. The emotions were strangled in his throat. Charlie lifted his gaze from the ground to hold my eyes and there was only one word to describe his look: sorrow. Overwhelming, all-encompassing sorrow. I pulled him close and pressed my cheek against his right ear and he bent his forehead onto my shoulder.

For better or for worse. In sickness and in health.

We stayed pressed together for a few moments and then, Charlie lifted his head slightly and whispered into my cheek, "I feel like I have just been told that an assassin has boarded a bus with a loaded gun. I just don't know which route he took, so I don't know how long it is going to take for him to get here to kill me."

Over the next few months, that thought haunted me daily. It was a silent soundtrack of fear running in the background of my brain every day. I would be standing in the kitchen staring into the refrigerator unsure why I had opened the door. I would be reading a book but realize I had been rereading the same paragraph never turning the page. I would be driving only to discover I could not remember my destination. That is how I ended up taking a walk that would begin to reframe how I saw everything in our lives.

On my way to our neighborhood shopping center, I realized I had forgotten what my original errand had been. At the stoplight, I saw a small church with a small sign I had never noticed: Sacred Garden. Inexplicably drawn toward it, my hands turned the steering wheel toward the sign and into the church parking lot. Once out of my car, I could see hidden behind some azalea bushes was the focal point of this garden—a labyrinth.

It was a large circular design with the path created by gray stones set into the grass. I had read a little about labyrinths in some of my new books, so I was not a complete stranger to this idea. I knew that unlike a maze, there are no dead ends in a labyrinth. There are no tricks in the turns. If I followed the path, it was designed to lead me to the center and then back out. Curious, I took my first few steps forward, but just as quickly, the path turned away. To follow, I had to walk farther and farther away from center. It felt frustrating to be so close yet moving away from where I knew was the goal: a center rosette. Looking up from my tan-and-blue espadrilles, I tried to see the path. It seemed so simple— right in front of me—but every time my eyes searched for the way, it was hidden in the twist ahead. The gray pavers marked a clear path, yet there was no way to guess or predict the route. I had to trust that the labyrinth maker would lead me to the center.

My need for control, to know the plan and solve this puzzle, was clear—I wanted to be in charge of my path. It was no different in life. I wanted to know how it would all turn out. I wanted to know when this medical mystery would end. Would Charlie have another heart attack but this time not survive? This time, a different nurse: *We are sorry, he didn't make it.*

When would that be? How much longer? How much time did we have?

Refocusing, I exhaled into the April air. In the spring, all of Charlotte blossoms into the most dazzling array of dogwoods, azaleas, and cherry trees. The sixty-foot majestic pin oaks erupt into a vibrant green and the gray wood of winter disappears creating a lush canopy overhead. With all my worries of Charlie, I hadn't noticed this year. I hadn't seen that spring had sprung because in my heart and head, it was still a bleak, wintry gray.

With each step I took, slowly trusting the path in front of me, I noticed. There were pink azaleas in full bloom around me. I could feel the vice grip in my chest releasing slightly. For the first time in four months, I forgot that I was afraid. I stopped trying to find all the answers, I just breathed and walked. One foot after the other. Spiraling peacefully to the center. Closing my eyes, I could hear the rustle of the trees whispering to me. It felt as if the wind and all of the garden was giving me a gentle hug. *You are okay,* it whispered. *Here, you are okay.*

With my eyes closed, I forgot that I was in a church garden and I was simply in prayer. Asking for help. My rational mind knew there were no viable medical answers but my soul needed some solutions. *Life plan*, I thought. I need to know *my life plan*. *Please God, tell me the plan*. I need to know how this awful movie ends.

No, the wind seemed to whisper to me. *Life path*. You just need to follow your *life path*.

One foot in front of the other. The next right step. Take the next right step. Trust the path.

When I reached the center, I sank to the stones. Sitting cross-legged on the ground I could feel the warmth through my blue jeans and into my fingertips resting on the ground. My large exhale came out naturally without any yoga instructor present to tell me to try or notice my breath. It was my own exhale of exhaustion.

I realized I was crying. Just gentle wet salt sliding down my cheeks. Part sadness for what it seemed we had lost. Part relief in releasing control. Part fear of what was to come.

I don't know how long I remained in the center, eyes closed, but when I opened my eyes the green of the garden reminded me of the world outside that I would return to. The gray in my head felt like a fog finally lifting. I took the first three steps out and turned hard left to begin winding my way out of the labyrinth.

As I walked each of the eleven concentric circles and took each of the thirty-four turns, I held a momentary peace in my center. Returning to the world outside the labyrinth, I knew that this was the feeling I needed to recover. A way to wake up each day in this world with all of my fears, yet still trusting the path in front of me.

I didn't fully understand my experience in the sacred garden until I read Laurie Goodstein's *New York Times* article, "Reviving Labyrinths, Paths to Inner Peace." In it she wrote how many Americans are searching "beyond the church pulpit for spiritual experience and solace." In doing so, they "have rediscovered the labyrinth," which is an ancient way to connect to the divine. Walking through the circular path of a labyrinth offers the seeker a way to slow down, concentrate simply on the next step and contemplate their emotions.

Goodstein credits the rise of popularity of labyrinths in the United States to one priest in San Francisco, Reverend Lauren Artress.

"When you walk into the labyrinth," Ms. Artress said in an interview, "the mind quiets, and then you begin to see through what's happening inside. You become transparent to yourself. You can see that you're scared, or frightened, or that you lack courage."

Stumbling into the garden labyrinth that day, I didn't know about Reverend Artress or the ancient history. Ever since the Middle Ages, labyrinths had been predictably leading walkers to the center and returning them to the world.

Almost thirty years before, Reverend Artress had an epiphany of her own walking a labyrinth while on retreat. Beginning with her own Grace Cathedral in San Francisco, she re-created the complex sacred geometry from the Chartres labyrinth in France onto the stone floor of a California church. Through workshops and walks, Artress, a priest and psychotherapist, built bridges between the traditional church and nontraditional forms of spirituality. In her book, *Walking a Sacred Path: Rediscovering the Labyrinth as a Spiritual Practice*, Reverend Artress writes:

> *I moved from curiosity to skepticism to profound respect for the uncanny gifts of insight, wisdom and peace the labyrinth offers. It connects us to the depths of our souls so we can remember who we are*

Over three decades, Reverend Artress developed a three-step process now widely used for walking a labyrinth: Releasing, Receiving, Returning. It begins with "Releasing:" as you step onto the path you symbolically shed your worries which prepare you for the next phase. Upon reaching the center, you are "Receiving:" pausing to reflect on insights gained from your walk. As you leave, you are "Returning:" taking what you have learned back into the world.

This threefold path—Releasing, Receiving, Returning—I had just experienced in the church garden. It would not only teach me a lesson that day but serve as the larger metaphor for the seven-year journey I had unknowingly entered through the new door of Charlie's rare disease. I was definitely feeling spiritually homeless and needed to find a way home. The life plan I believed I could so carefully craft and control was obliterated. My only way forward was to try to find trust in a life path when I could not see around the next turn.

I had to believe as Reverend Artress assured, *"The labyrinth offers a spiritual exercise that becomes the path of life. It allows the wandering soul to find a way to center, to find a way home."*

It is this brief shimmer of what is possible that we crave in hopeless places. When we have fallen so far that can't see any way out, we need reminders that thinking and feeling differently is possible. This momentary glimpse allows us to trust, moving forward on the path before us—even if it means crawling on our knees.

RELEASING

AND MAYBE THIS IS WHAT FAITH IS ALL ABOUT—having a way to understand and accept and endure the most incomprehensible things that happened to us. Having faith didn't have to mean subscribing to a certain set of religious beliefs or praying to a deity or going through elaborate rituals in a church or temple or mosque. Maybe it meant surrendering the complete control we assume we have over our lives, and instead opening to the idea that another force, benevolent and mysterious, looked after us. Maybe it means practicing acceptance of whatever life brings our way. And maybe it also meant remembering that our sorrows and joys, just like our bodies, were temporary.

DR. SUNITA PURI
*That Good Night: Life and Medicine
in the Eleventh Hour*

5
SEEKING

ANSWERS ALREADY
WAITING TO BE FOUND

Walking the labyrinth and looking for new answers began a process of filling that inner sinkhole I had felt for so long. While I couldn't find medical answers on the Internet for Charlie, I started Googling for hope. I was seeking instruction for this new life path where I could not see the way forward, yet I had to learn to trust in where I might be going.

If Charlie had not survived, I would have been groping my way through the shelves of "Grief and Bereavement," "Widowhood," or "Love and Loss." But thankfully, Charlie was very much alive and I wasn't seeking to hasten my way through the next terrifying doorway surely waiting for me: Bereavement. Charlie and I were simply "Waiting for Disaster," "Living with the Incurable," and "Hoping for a Way Out," none of which seemed to be a searchable genre.

The more I read, the more I realized that my spiritual emergency caused by medical emergency was not unique to me. Searching for spiritual answers after trauma is a human certainty. While we can easily cope without spirituality when life is going well, it is the inevitable, blindsiding events that bring us to our knees seeking divine rescue. In their article, "Living with Mortality, Life Goes On," Stanford researchers, Malin Dollinger, M.D., and Bernard Dubrow, M.S., write about "The

Five Stages of Living with Mortality" all patients go through after a new and difficult diagnosis. Dollinger and Dubrow ask:

> *But what happens when we are jolted by the diagnosis of a possibly fatal illness such as cancer? After recoiling from the shocking news and accepting its reality, how can we cope with this new state of uncertainty? How can we adjust our lifelong attitudes and renew our trust in the future? For the first time, we find ourselves in the strange and disruptive situation of having to cope with living and dying at the same time. How can we do it?*

It was exactly what Charlie and I were experiencing: *"coping with living and dying at the same time."* Swinging through a roller coaster of emotions from, "I can't believe Charlie lived!" to "I can't believe this can happen again!"

Dollinger and Dubrow described five stages all those living with mortality experience: Disbelief, Discovery, Redirection, Resolution, and Affirmation. We had already moved through "Disbelief," reeling from Charlie's initial diagnosis. "Discovery" was also behind us as there were no more answers to be found about Spontaneous Coronary Artery Dissection. No more specialists to see and no treatment to be found. We were clearly in stage three, "Redirection," which the Stanford researchers describe as *"when people must adapt, or reimagine their lives given a new understanding of their own mortality through new circumstance."*

Living with my unrelenting fears about Charlie dying from another dissection with no possibility for remission, I was clearly inhabiting this new phase of Redirection in my life. Only much later would I realize this phase was very much like my labyrinth walk and the threefold path— Releasing, Receiving, and Returning—described by Reverend Lauren Artress. I would have to *release* old ideas about how I believed my life, and Charlie's life, would unfold. And somehow, I needed to *receive* some advice or wisdom that would help me *return* to living in a new way with a new perspective.

There was no way to go back to complacent living, before I knew that arteries could, without warning, split. There was no way to bring back a life or love you have lost or restore health you might have taken for granted. But with new understanding, we can learn to live differently.

At the time, I didn't understand any of that. All I knew was that I felt rudderless with no faith strong enough to withstand the waves of bad news that kept crashing over us. I had questions I didn't even know how to ask, much less seek answers for.

It turns out, Charlie's dad, who the girls called "Poppop," would be my best teacher for finding answers to difficult questions.

Before Charlie's heart attack, it was Poppop's heart we all worried about. Over his lifetime, Charlie's dad had his own cardiac issues so it was unfathomable to think that his son had almost predeceased him. When Poppop first reunited with Charlie after our traumatic ICU stay, he pulled Charlie close for a full chest-to-chest hug. In this embrace, Poppop's aging heart beat beside Charlie's stented heart. With his wispy white hair and his eyes pressed tight under his clear spectacles, Poppop couldn't speak. There are no words to tell your son how grateful you are not to be attending his funeral.

Watching them, I ached for my own father. I wanted my dad to hold me and reassure me that everything was going to be all right. Growing up, my father had always been my source of strength and I was devastated to lose him to leukemia when he was only sixty-four years old. At the time I was a thirty-five-year-old mom and I could not fully appreciate just how young sixty-four was. Witnessing Charlie receive the needed embrace from his eighty-eight-year-old father, it struck me how many years were stolen from my dad. Even worse, Charlie was barely fifty-three, which meant it was possible he could die almost a decade younger than my father.

This realization that Charlie might not have much time left fueled my need to make the most of all our time together. With our daughters each working or away at school, that first Christmas holiday after Charlie's heart attack would be even more precious. I found a resort hotel that had passed Dr. Hayes's criteria: close proximity to a cardiac catherization hospital. I was determined to make it the perfect Christmas for the six of us after a year of constant worry.

It was on the very first day of our carefully planned vacation, stretched out by the pool, when Charlie received the call. He had picked up his cell and moved away to sit on steps of the shallow end of the pool. Although I could not hear what he was saying, Charlie's expression was somber. Assuming it was simply a work crisis, I turned back to my magazine. A few moments later, I glanced up to see Charlie was off the phone but he seemed paralyzed. Holding his head in his hands, Charlie was staring past the turquoise pool water to the ocean horizon. Rising from my lounge chair, I nestled beside him on the steps. Our feet dangled next to each other in the water barely touching ankles. "Everything ok?" I asked.

"It's Poppop," Charlie said choking on the words. "He's in the hospital. It's not good."

Lauren, Kailey, Emma, and Maddie went from basking in bikinis to sobbing poolside. Over the next twelve hours, our initial worry devolved into a full-blown crisis. Poppop was not expected to make it through the night. A whirlwind of calls cancelled our vacation as we desperately searched for six seats to New York amidst the impossibly packed holiday flights. We all needed to say one last goodbye.

Forty-eight hours after we began our Christmas vacation, we landed in New York City. A taxi brought us to the Manhattan hospital a little after 9:00 p.m. on December 23, 2013. Circling Poppop's ICU bed, the scene was eerily similar to ten months prior when the girls had arrived late at night around Charlie's ICU bed in Lowell, Massachusetts, only ten months before. Poppop was unmoving with tubes and an EKG monitor beeping steadily beside him. His breathing was labored through his partly open mouth and his eyes remained closed. We were not sure if he could hear us, or if he even knew we were there, but one by one, we each held Poppop's hand to say goodbye to the only remaining grandfather in our lives.

When it was Charlie's turn, the girls and I stepped outside to give the father and son privacy.

Through the glass, I watched Charlie whisper his last words to the man he loved and respected the most in the world. I could see Charlie's profile bending close to his father's face. I wanted for Poppop to open his eyes and give one more smile, one more glimpse of the dear man who called his granddaughters "dreamy." I don't know what Charlie said to his dad, but when he came out, his face was crumpled and crying. We formed a circle around Charlie, holding tight to each other and to all the memories of the man who had started our family.

The next morning on Christmas Eve, Poppop left this world a little after 9:00 a.m.

I thought there could not be a worse day for someone to die because I thought it would have to be just the worst Christmas in our worst year. Even though her husband of more than five decades died that morning, Granny insisted that the family cook our traditional roast beef, mashed potatoes, and green bean feast that night.

"No one feels like eating," I hissed to Charlie as we peeled potatoes in Granny's cramped kitchen bursting with Izards. In the adjacent den, I could see our daughters curled against each other, sorrowfully looking through photo albums remembering their beloved, bespectacled grandfather who smiled sweetly back at them from the pages.

"It's what Granny wants," Charlie shrugged.

In a year when none of Charlie's family of five siblings, spouses, and children had planned to be together for the holidays, we were magically assembled around the mahogany dinner table in the Izard family home. Last-minute plane rides and long car trips had instantly been arranged within hours of Poppop's death so that twenty of us were pressed shoulder to shoulder joining in a Christmas Eve blessing. As unlikely as it had seemed to make dinner a normal Christmas, that traditional feast was the one gift we all needed. To be gathered together. To remember the man who began this family. To laugh about his quirks and to marvel at his strengths.

Twenty-family-members strong, we crowded unexpectedly around the dining table to honor the man we lost and to hold tight his memory among us. We lingered that evening telling stories and raising our glasses toasting to how Poppop called our four daughters "the girlies." How he swam a million pool laps in slow, methodic strokes. How he always wore his overcoat at the dinner table because Granny insisted on keeping a chilly house to save money on heating bills. How at every meal except this one, Poppop would always be the last Izard to put down his fork and declare, "That was the best meal I've had since yesterday!"

Days later at his memorial service, I discovered something I never knew about Poppop: he had been on a lifelong spiritual quest. While I knew my father-in-law faithfully attended the local Episcopalian church, I didn't know Poppop was also intently seeking answers to deep theological questions. At his service, the priest talked about how Poppop had signed up for a course called, "Education for Ministry."

This "EfM" class was not merely a bible study, it was a true commitment to delve into life's most profound questions. Participants commit to a three-year course with weekly reading assignments and study sessions to learn about God. During this intense seminar, participants come to understand the entire scope of the Christian tradition from the earliest period to the present.

At Poppop's funeral, the Episcopal priest delivered an eloquent eulogy along with a surprise. As she spoke from the pulpit, the priest shook her head in disbelief, telling the hundreds of mourners that in her whole career, she had never known anyone to take EfM more than once. Her eyes lit up and her smile gave away her punch line as she let us all know, "Bob Izard was on his fourth course."

At this news, the gathered friends and family smiled, shaking our collective heads in amazement. *Four times?* Why would Poppop sign up for EfM four times? That is twelve years of study in total. Seminary for ordained ministers is typically only three years. Our Poppop, at eighty-eight years old, was beginning his twelfth year of study when he died.

"He told me he wanted to get it right," the priest said. "Bob said he still had a question and he needed to find the answer. I told him it was okay to stop. I wanted to give him an exit ramp off this spiritual highway!"

She laughed as she recounted his persistence. There was still one answer Poppop was determined to find. That was why he kept signing up over and over. He still needed one final answer.

The priest let us all contemplate that for a moment before she told us the rest of the story. On December 23, the day before Poppop died, she had visited him in the hospital. She must have been with him sometime in the daylight hours before our family arrived late at night to encircle his bed. Although he was semiconscious by the time we arrived at his hospital bed, Poppop had apparently spoken lucidly to this priest just hours earlier.

"I think I have it," Poppop whispered to her. "I finally have the answer,"

After living eighty-eight years and studying intensely for the last twelve of them, Poppop finally received his one last and wondrous answer. During the rest of the service, that is all I could think about.

On our way out of the sanctuary, I tugged on Charlie's gray suit sleeve. "Did you know that story?"

Charlie shook his head. "I knew he was doing some kind of study with his church but I had no idea what it was."

"I wish I had," I told Charlie. "I wish I had known to ask Poppop what the answer was."

"I wish I had known to ask him what the question was," Charlie said. "That's what really matters. What was his twelve-year question?"

After that, I began seeking in earnest. Rather than happening upon books, I sought volumes that might touch upon not so much the answers, but the questions I should be asking. One book had been waiting on my shelf for years, just waiting for me to notice it.

Don Davidson was a family friend who our girls referred to as their "third grandfather." Don and his wife, Anne, had been regularly coming to our home for Thanksgiving and Christmas for at least ten years. Every time they arrived for dinner, Don brought a book. He had a closet in his home full of them—not used ones but brand-new paperbacks he bought in bulk of his favorite titles. Don didn't give away mysteries or thrillers. Don gave away spiritual wisdom which he steadfastly believed everyone in this world could use more of.

For years, Don had been writing notes on the inside covers of books he wanted Charlie and me to read. Apparently, Don was in a hurry to speed along our religious education. But with four kids to raise and careers to pursue, Charlie and I hadn't made much time for reading Don's not-so-subtly suggested titles. At the time, I was still reading novels to escape and Charlie preferred business books. So we had always smiled sweetly at Don, thanked him profusely for his book gifts but shelved his offerings unopened.

After Poppop's funeral, I knew exactly where I could start looking for advice on my own twelve-year questions—with Don's favorite, Frederick Buechner. Over the years, Don had given us at least six Buechner books and it was easy to find one of them as they were sprinkled throughout our den bookcases.

Opening up *Listening to Your Life: Daily Meditations with Frederick Buechner*, I read what Don had written on the title page:

To Charlie and Kathy
Hoping this will offer some meaningful insights
and with all good wishes,
Don

As I began reading, tears filled my eyes. Page after page spoke directly to my current fears and questions. I wondered if Don's angel spirit was watching me now, years after he pressed this book into my hands, finally receiving his message. Somehow, he must have sensed my spiritual homelessness and his gifts of just the right words waiting patiently to help me find my way home.

In this, one of his best-selling titles, *Listening to Your Life*, Buechner wrote:

Listen to your life. See it for the fathomless mystery it is. In the boredom and pain of it, no less than in the excitement and gladness: touch, taste, smell your way to the holy and hidden heart of it, because in the last analysis all moments are key moments, and life itself is grace.

I may not have known what questions I should be asking in this life. It may have taken a heart attack and a rare disease to begin asking them. But once I started seeking, the answers were all around me—just waiting to be found.

6

CONNECTING

THE CURRENT OF GRACE
HEALING US ALL

While I desperately wanted to begin "listening to my life" as Buechner suggested, I was still stuck in the hopelessness of our situation. It seemed I was wading through what Dr. Elisabeth Kübler-Ross writes about in her best-selling book, *On Grief and Grieving: Finding the Meaning of Grief Through the Five Stages of Loss.* Her research show us there are Five Stages of Grief: Denial, Anger, Bargaining, Depression, and Acceptance. I felt clearly mired in Stage 4 (Depression), with no clear path toward Stage 5 (Acceptance). While Charlie had survived, whatever certainty I had about life had died. With SCAD lurking in our future, we had no way to plan and no way to predict. It left me feeling unbalanced and unable to move forward. Who knew when we might next be racing to the hospital? Who could say if the next dissection might be fatal?

When tragedies strike, we can spend a lot of time wandering with our pain. There is no timeline for grief. No clock that should tell us when time runs out on mourning our losses and when we should move through our sadness. It is different for each of us and different for every type of bereavement.

Dr. Joanne Cacciatore, PhD, is an associate professor and researcher at Arizona State University in Trauma and Bereavement. She has studied and published widely on traumatic grief, loss, and illness and continues to work with those who are mired in grief. In her book, *Bearing the Unbearable: Love, Loss, and the Heartbreaking Path of Grief,* Dr. Cacciatore writes about her work with people who have lost those they love—spouses, children, parents—and how the process is unique for each person and each relationship. Her work is both an academic interest and intensely personal after experiencing the loss of her baby daughter. Dr. Cacciatore researches and writes poignantly about death and loss to help others:

> *Being the mother of a child who has died is a tragic privilege—*
> *one for which I never asked and certainly never wanted.*
>
> *Yet here I am—and here you are—unbearably wounded.*
>
> *It is the bereaved who are awakened from the slumber of*
> *self-satisfaction.*
>
> *It is the bereaved who can heal our world.*

To be clear, I had not experienced anything as tragic as Dr. Cacciatore or anyone who has lost a child or spouse. Yet the upending of the life Charlie and I knew did feel as if I had been awakened from a slumber of certainty. I needed to begin living again—accepting what is controllable and what is not. I could not find Charlie a better doctor. We already had the best. I could not Google a cure. There was not one to be found. I could not receive assurances about which day might be our last day together. No one is afforded that luxury. Instead of worrying about the future, there was really only one question I should be asking: If I knew today was our last day together, how would I live?

In the first year and a half after Charlie's diagnosis, I had spent so much of my time alone in my own head chasing the unknowable. I had allowed myself to imagine that Charlie and I might be the only ones suffering with the anxiety of uncertainty. There was this wallowing I needed to allow myself before I tired of it and was ready to re-engage with the world. When I finally looked up from our own sadness, I realized connecting with others was the obvious way to no longer feel alone.

Although many of our friends were handling health challenges with their parents—dementia, cancer or broken hips—few couples our age were dealing with their own health crises. I was forty-nine and Charlie fifty-three, so few friends were navigating a rare disease like his. One couple living with a difficult diagnosis, however, was Sally and Steve.

Steve had been undergoing treatment for an illness only to discover too late that it was an aggressive cancer. We didn't understand how serious it had become until I received an email from a priest at our church, Reverend Lisa Saunders. Like so many of us, Lisa wanted to do something for Sally and Steve even though medically, there was nothing more to be done. Lisa had read an article about a neighborhood that rallied around a friend like Steve to support him near the end of his life. His friends had wrapped him in love literally, by becoming a human ribbon around the man's home to pray for their dying friend. That is exactly what Reverend Saunders wanted us to do for Steve. Lisa's email invited friends to gather the next afternoon at Steve and Sally's home to encircle their home with love and prayer.

Since Charlie and I lived just around the corner from Sally and Steve, we walked the long block toward their home the next afternoon. The winter February day was sunny but bitterly cold. When we turned the corner to approach their home, dozens of people were already gathered on the lawn with more friends still arriving. The normally bright Southern greeting of "Hey!" was replaced with silent nods, creating a somber atmosphere.

By the time, Reverend Saunders arrived, there were well over a hundred people huddled in coats, gloves, and hats on the suburban lawn. It looked as if we might be assembled for a protest and, maybe, in some ways it was. A protest that this was happening to this kind family. A protest that this should not be happening to this good man. A protest that too often, life is simply not fair.

Lisa passed out pages with hymns on them and explained what we were about to do. We would stretch ourselves into a band of friends around the house and lift up Steve and Sally in our collective love. Beginning with the first two songs on the sheet, we would walk clockwise around the home so that everyone would get a chance to wave to Steve as he rested on a hospital bed near a back window. His family gathered by his side for this service to celebrate their sweet father, husband, brother, and son.

Charlie and I began on the front lawn, so it was almost thirty minutes before we rotated to where we would finally greet Steve and his family. I don't remember the songs we sang or the prayers we murmured in unison. I only remember that when we finally made it near the garden window to see Steve, some improvisation to Lisa's planned service had begun.

Through the singing and praying together, the somber mood had lifted and we were all feeling a part of something so much bigger. The power of being with over one hundred people gathered in the common cause of loving a great friend had buoyed everyone present that afternoon. Sally and Steve felt the collective joy as well, waving and smiling at each guest. Someone, knowing Steve's love for the Carolina Tarheels, began singing the UNC-Chapel Hill fight song and we all joined in. The prayer circle had given way to a pep rally for life. This life that we were living together with shared joys and shared sorrows. We all understood that our fight songs and enthusiasm could not carry us to a win. A few days later, Steve would still lose his battle with cancer. But on that chilly afternoon, we were all fully present to behold something really good in the world.

Being a part of that band of love caused a shift in me. It was the closest I have ever come to attending a revival. While our prayers and hymns had not saved Steve's life, it began to release the vice grip of fear I had surrounding death—not only about Charlie's, but my own. Witnessing that circle of friends and Steve's smiling face waving out the window granted to me a peace I still carry. We had shown up to give something to Steve and like all holy moments, we received infinite grace in return.

I believe there was an underlying question for probably everyone on that lawn. As friends of Steve and Sally, we all had hoped to be part of a very different celebration. We all wanted to rejoice in a miraculous cure. We had all prayed for the doctors to be wrong. We all truly hoped for a last-minute Hail Mary healing. For an intervention from God in order for Steve to survive because we all had prayed faithfully for it to be so.

It happens every time we hear of damning diagnoses, and it seems to happen to the friends we feel least deserving of medical death sentences. The glioblastomas and the Stage IV spreading cancers that ravage human brains and mortal bodies. We close our eyes and fervently pray to a God we hope is listening.

In 2016, CNN reported on a study about prayer with surprising results. The study conducted by Jeff Levin, Institute for Studies of Religion, Baylor University, showed that nearly 90% of Americans had prayed for healing for others and over 80% had prayed for healing for themselves. Levin told CNN in an interview:

"Outside of belief in God, healing prayer might be the most ubiquitous religious practice that there is," Levin said. "This might be

one of the most prevalent forms of primary care medicine, and I
don't say that lightly."

One of the most prayed-for patients in recent memory was thirty-
seven-year-old best-selling author, Rachel Held Evans, whose writing
connected with millions of readers wrestling with their faith. Among
Rachel's many followers were thousands who felt betrayed by the conservative Christian communities in which they were raised. Rachel wrote
about creating a different kind of church—one that was inclusive not
exclusive. In each of her four books, Rachel encouraged readers from
agnostics to lapsed evangelicals to re-engage with a God who she knew
to be a much more loving deity than is often sold in Sunday "sinner"
sermons. In the spring of 2019, however, Rachel was hospitalized from
a brain infection which caused seizures. When the word of her illness
spread though social media, literally thousands of readers began praying
for her recovery.

When Rachel Held Evans was placed in a medically induced coma,
so many people were desperately hoping for a medical miracle that the
hashtag, #prayforRHE, began trending on Twitter. Sadly, just like our
friend Steve, the prayers were not answered in the way friends had
hoped. Rachel Held Evans passed away on May 4, 2019, devastating so
many who were inspired by her words.

"I keep hoping it's a nightmare from which I'll awake," her husband,
Daniel Evans said in a statement. "Rachel's presence in this world was a
gift to us all, and her work will long survive her."

Prominent deaths like Rachel Held Evans' and less known but
equally devastating deaths like Steve's are each cases that defy what we
want to believe to be true. Steve was a good, good man and we wanted
him to have a longer life to experience his two sons become grown men.
Rachel was a good, good woman and thus, she deserved a longer life
to keep connecting people of all faiths to something they could believe

in. Rachel Held Evans left behind words that could ultimately comfort those most devastated by her death. In the last blog post she would ever write, "Lent for the Lamenting," Rachel posted this:

> *Death is a part of life. My prayer for you this season is that you make time to celebrate that reality, and to grieve that reality, and that you will know you are not alone.*

Rachel Held Evans understood well the difference between curing and healing. In her book *Searching for Sunday: Loving, Leaving, and Finding the Church*, Rachel wrote:

> *But there is a difference between curing and healing, and I believe the church is called to the slow and difficult work of healing. We are called to enter into one another's pain, anoint it as holy, and stick around no matter the outcome.*

The Band of Love around Steve's home—it was its own kind of healing. The online prayer circle united in #prayforRHE—it was its own kind of healing. The kind of healing needed for those of us left behind devastated by the death of someone we hold dear. The kind of healing that awakens us from a slumber of certainty. The kind of healing needed to remember that we are here with each other to connect and become communities, which will hold each other close no matter the outcomes. That kind of healing that is found not only with each other but through the current of grace running through this world healing us all.

7

AWAKENING

THE CHOICE TO LIVE
IN FAITH NOT FEAR

With unwanted diagnoses come doctors and, usually, too many of them. Suddenly, medical buildings we never knew existed become part of our daily life along with the nurses and medical professionals inside them. We begin to spend countless hours in waiting rooms. It is a new kind of purgatory. Time spent making appointments, attending consultations and treatments, awaiting results, receiving new information, process-ing shifting prognoses. Navigating this disease world, it helps to have a quarterback for all the recommended treatment—one doctor who you trust implicitly to be honest and always in your corner. When Charlie was diagnosed with SCAD, we realized we were going to need the very best doctor in Charlotte and one name came to my mind immediately: Dr. Jane Harrell.

I had met "Dr. Jane" as she is known, because she directed the free medical clinic at the Urban Ministry Center. We were colleagues of sorts because I was on staff as the director of a housing program and Dr. Jane provided care for those living on the streets. Initially, I thought that was the extent of her practice but I later discovered Dr. Jane was a highly sought-after general practitioner in Charlotte.

Only a few inches over five feet tall, Jane is a tiny, blonde ball of energy, always wearing her uniform of baggy blue scrubs. With her pixie face and infinitely patient bedside manner, Dr. Jane had earned the respect of even the gruffest guests in our soup kitchen. Most endearing of all, Dr. Jane always delivered her diagnosis with a little bit of divine. "Don't you worry about this bronchitis, Sam. God's got you."

Jane possessed an unwavering and unpreachy brand of faith that was intriguing to me since I was still wrestling with what I believed. With her easy and frequent mentions of God, I wasn't sure how Jane and Charlie would get along; but to survive with SCAD, I knew Charlie needed the best possible medical care. Jane had a full patient load but when I called to explain Charlie's diagnosis she made an immediate appointment available.

After his first visit, I asked Charlie, "What did you think?"

"She is an amazing listener," Charlie said as he continued to sort mail at his desk on our sunporch. "She asked me about everything—we talked for over an hour."

That was unusual in itself. Charlie never told long-winded stories. If I wanted details, I always had to dig for them so I pressed, "What else?"

Charlie seemed to be considering the question as his gaze shifted from the junk mail to the framed photos on his desk. There were many family pictures, but my favorite was taken at a dude ranch several summers before. In the ten-year-old photo, Charlie is lying flat on his stomach atop a log bench with his mouth wide open in laughter from the weight of all four daughters piled on top of him. Our twins, Emma and Maddie, are balancing precariously at the peak of the pyramid about to tumble to the ground. Charlie seemed to be studying this favorite family memory.

He finally answered, "She told me I should think about what brings me joy."

"Really? Jane used the word *joy*?" That was hardly a word used in standard-issue medical language.

Charlie nodded. "She asked if what I was doing with my life was bringing me joy."

As he spoke, Charlie studied another photo, this one of Emmitt, our beloved corgi, who died a year ago. Typically, corgis have two perky ears, but Emmitt had one that continually flopped over which had given him the permanent look of a puppy. In the black-and-white image, Emmitt is perched on our backyard bench gazing thoughtfully back at the camera.

"I realized so many of the things that I loved I can't do anymore," Charlie said.

It was true. Charlie could no longer test his physical limits either, jumping out of helicopters or even at the gym. All the things that had brought him so much joy in this world were now off-limits. The heli-skiing. The tennis. The running. The adventure. It was as if everything he had ever loved now had a poison-warning label across it: risk of imminent death. Charlie had been forced to make a complete conversion from choosing activities precisely because they were risky to avoiding them at all cost for that same very reason.

Shifting his gaze to the backyard, Charlie contemplated our trees. There were four sixty-foot oaks shading our yard, creating a full canopy over our two-story red brick home. When our dog, Emmitt, was alive, Charlie used to wander through the oaks and azaleas picking weeds while our little corgi pranced behind him like a tiny parade of one.

"Did Jane talk much about God?" I asked.

"Not specifically. She just mentioned a scripture I should look up," he said.

I smiled at the idea of Charlie, my pragmatist, receiving such theological advice from his doctor. "Which one?"

He smiled like a boy who had forgotten his homework, "I don't know. I didn't write it down."

That year, the second year of living with SCAD, Dr. Jane began saving both our lives. I have no idea how many phone calls she fielded from me as well as Charlie. The first year after his dissection, the calls were more medical than mental. But that second year, the calls were more about our unrelenting fear. With time, medical mystery takes an emotional toll on patients and caregivers through the pure psychic stress. There is a radical uncertainty that comes with any new diagnosis but particularly with a rare disease. The lack of research, support groups, treatment, and reliable prognosis all make the future completely unpredictable.

Charlie once asked Jane, "What percentage of your practice is about physical healthcare and what percentage is about mental healthcare?"

"Sometimes I feel 80% mental health," she answered.

For what ailed the body, Dr. Jane relied on medical science. For what ailed the mind, Dr. Jane often prescribed God. Charlie and I both became her patients and Dr. Jane often sent encouragement to me, the caregiver. It was not unusual to receive a text from her that read simply "Jeremiah 29:11-12" followed by a rainbow emoji. Since I was not well-versed in theology, I always had to Google Jane's Bible verses to understand her cryptic messages but it was always a message of love and encouragement. That was just Dr. Jane.

As for her struggling patient, Charlie began to be buoyed by Dr. Jane's theologically laced wisdom as well. After another visit to discuss his own mortality as well as the death of his father, Charlie smiled as he recounted Jane's blunt spiritual advice.

"She said, 'Charlie, let's face it. You should be dead but you are not. So you have to decide. Are you going to live your life in fear or are you going to live your life in faith?'"

That really was the core of our problem. We were living purely out of fear. We were paralyzed with day-to-day worries of Charlie's mortality and we were finding it difficult to move past them. Attending Poppops's funeral made me feel as if I was practicing for Charlie's service. Seeing all of his family gathered for the memorial service felt like the preview of when we might assemble next for another good, Izard man.

From the beginning of Charlie's cardiac issues, I thought the best plan for his health would be a different career. Charlie had a demanding job in the financial sector that required constant, weekly commuting between New York and Charlotte. In the first hours and days after his heart attack, it felt like a clear sign we should radically alter our lives and make new choices given Charlie's new diagnosis. After his life-altering event, I wanted to dream different dreams.

"Maybe you could quit and do something you love like coach lacrosse?" I said.

"Or teach?" Charlie said. "I have always thought I might like to teach history or politics."

Giddy with new chances and new possibilities, we considered even a more radical lifestyle change—like moving to Montana or Wyoming, which had always been a shared dream. But after that first year, we had gone back to doing exactly what we had been doing. All that initial talk about dreaming different dreams had passed. Charlie was slogging through each day with what seemed to me a depression seeping to his core now that he couldn't vigorously exercise. Running and sweating used to be his best strategies for clearing his head.

"Maybe you should talk to someone," I hinted, meaning a therapist.

"I do," Charlie answered. "I talk to you and Jane."

While I could not persuade Charlie to talk to a therapist, I became convinced what he needed was a therapy dog. Not a dog actually trained for therapy, just a four-legged friend to replace our corgi, Emmitt. With no dog and four almost-grown daughters, our very quiet house felt too much like museum. Maybe a puppy would be exactly what Charlie

needed to get him excited about his monotonous walks around the block
and reinvigorated about his life.

What brings you joy Charlie?

For weeks I had been researching breeders, but when I found what
I thought was the perfect puppy, Charlie took a lot of convincing. On a
weekend visit to a friend's farm, a pair of black Lab puppies came tumbling out of the barn to greet us. We learned there was one more puppy,
a male, from the same championship litter still waiting for a home.

Cradling one of the adorable fur balls, I raised my eyebrows hope-
fully at Charlie but he shook his head. "We don't need a champion Lab,"
Charlie said. "I don't even hunt."

That night, we went to a dinner party with our friends at a nearby
farm and the hostess had heard about my love of the Labs.

"I heard you want the last puppy," she said.

"I do," I told her. "But Charlie is not convinced."

"Don't you worry," she said smiling. "Charlie is sitting next to me
tonight. I've got this!"

I am not sure what all our hostess said that night at the other end
of the dinner table to persuade Charlie but she really only needed one
fact. After many hours and much red wine, Charlie came with the news.

"Did she tell you?" Charlie asked.

"Tell me what?" I asked, having no idea what he meant.

"This litter of puppies. Guess what the father's name is?" Charlie
asked. "Goose!"

He smiled as he told me, shaking his head. He knew I don't believe
in coincidences. To me the significant sire's name was the sure sign that
this last puppy was meant for our home. And he was.

Dexter, named for Charlie's beloved grandfather, came to live with us
the next weekend and became Charlie's new best friend. While Dexter
was kindly attentive to me, he worshipped Charlie. Dexter seemed to
know instinctively that Charlie was his mission. His black tail went into

double-time pump action whenever Charlie was near and Dexter never tired of retrieving lacrosse balls in the park. When Charlie did his daily sit-ups, Dexter, ball in mouth, would sidle up quietly beside him. Then, Dexter would gently begin to climb on Charlie, straddling his chest with one paw resting on either side of Charlie's face. It's as if Dexter knew his job was to guard the damaged heart in Charlie's chest.

Just as Emmitt had before him, Dexter dutifully followed Charlie around the yard as he pulled weeds beneath the canopy of oaks in our backyard. Every weekend, with Dexter trotting beside him—a new yard parade of one. Charlie was beginning to rediscover what brought him joy.

On the weekends, Charlie and Dexter could take long walks together, but weekdays, exercising Dexter fell into my job jar. Monday through Friday, the promise of a daily walk was mine to keep. Even if I wanted to break the vow, Dexter would never let me.

His brown eyes begging me silently speaking, "Remember? Remember we have somewhere to go?"

Dexter developed his own game of how we would exercise together. Although I would begin by throwing the first pitch of his orange ball, Dexter controlled the rest. Dutifully retrieving the ball, he would then race ahead of me to hide the ball in the grass like an Easter egg waiting to be found. In case I could not see it, Dexter would move five to ten yards ahead of the ball in a full crouch remaining completely still except for his tail waving in frenzied anticipation. With his nose and front paws aimed at the waiting ball, Dexter always gave me, his human, a clear hint of where to retrieve next. In this game he developed, Dexter's job to was to hide, mine was to seek. We found a rhythm together in this routine, returning to the same park each day. Chasing the same ball. Walking in the same direction. Always clockwise. Always in the same circle.

At first, watching Dexter retrieve his ball allowed me to relax in small ways. It was difficult not to smile at his exuberance for this daily dance of purpose. I was envious of the single-minded passion and excitement Dexter found for his orange ball and his unending joy. There was something grounding about walking those daily circles under the same sixty-foot canopy of trees that made me feel my problems were small in comparison.

Eventually, I added music to our morning ritual. As soon as we were out of the car, my earphones went in. Dexter didn't play with other dogs and I didn't talk with other dog walkers. In the beginning, it was the country music from my Texas roots that played as we rounded each lap. Dixie Chicks. Jerry Jeff Walker. Willie Nelson. But much of that music didn't match my mood. I didn't want songs about trucks or mamas or getting drunk. I wanted songs about hope and life that could make me feel better about the daily fear I was living with. Just as I had moved from reading escape fiction to faith-filled nonfiction books, I needed some new melodies.

A random search on Spotify led me to *10,000 Reasons* by Matt Redman. Although I had never heard of him, I played the song anyway. As I walked and listened, I felt a peace I hadn't felt in a long time. So I played it again. And again. Finally, music to match my mood.

There was no promise in this lyric. No wishful thinking for a perfect outcome or a storybook ending. Just some hope and a reminder to appreciate this one day.

I found other songs by artists I never knew existed. Big Daddy Weave. Lauren Daigle. Zach Williams. I skipped and sorted to create my own perfect playlist and I realized there was a comfort in this New Age gospel music I couldn't quite explain.

Rain or shine, I began to look forward to our ritual not because Dexter needed it every day but because I did. The rhythm of walking the same place in the same direction. The music filling my soul. The pleasure in watching Dexter so exuberantly, obsessively, fulfill his life purpose. It became the one place I could think. The one place I could give up control. The one way I could breathe. Through this daily meditative, musical interlude in the park, I discovered my authentic way to calm. I thought the only church I had ever found was working with the homeless, where I lived faith in action. But in that park, I discovered my way to a spiritual connection could also be found under a Carolina sky, the air filled with the scent of magnolia blossoms and the sounds of soulful gospel music.

There are dozens of sixty-foot trees in that park, but one in particular has a massive trunk where one side of its undulating bark has a huge concave space large enough for an adult to curl inside. I found it almost by accident on a particular morning when Dexter had hidden his orange Easter egg right near the base of this hollow. As I stooped to fetch the ball, I saw this cave-like space and instead of picking up the ball, I paused to rest.

It felt like the first time I had sat down in almost two years. So many days of carrying the worry about Charlie's fragile heart. So many hours when the weight of being a widow at any given moment might crush me. Hidden in that hollow, I felt I wanted to just be swallowed up in that place. To hide from all that was happening at home. To not just walk in circles but to run back to a time before it all happened. To return to the time when I only worried about Charlie when he was heli-skiing and might fall in a tree well. Four days a year, I used to worry that Charlie would be buried by snow in the Canadian Rockies. Now, I just worried daily that I might have to bury him.

Sitting in that park pressed against a one-hundred-year-old tree, my worries were small and insignificant yet connected to something so much bigger. There was a peace in trying to have faith in that. A peace in releasing all that I could not control. I don't know how many clockwise circles it had taken or when exactly it had happened, but that park had become sacred ground for me. The combination of Dexter's joy, my music, the walking and the beauty of the trees had all combined to ground me in a very unexpected way. I discovered a peace in that park that had eluded me not only during Charlie's health crisis, but maybe my whole life.

Whether we knew it or not, Charlie and I had each finally stumbled upon finding a little peace each day that is a research-proven strategy. A July 2018 Harvard Health study advised patients under stress to "get back to nature."

"Many men are at higher risk for mood disorders as they age, from dealing with sudden life changes like health issues, the loss of loved ones, and even the new world of retirement," says Dr. Jason Strauss, director of geriatric psychiatry at Harvard-affiliated Cambridge Health Alliance. "They may not want to turn to medication or therapy for help, and for many, interacting with nature is one of the best self-improvement tools they can use."

Walking in nature lowers activity in the prefrontal cortex, a brain region that plays a part in constant, repetitive thoughts—especially ones that focus on negative emotions.

"When people are depressed or under high levels of stress, this part of the brain malfunctions, and people experience a continuous loop of negative thoughts," says Dr. Strauss.

My constant fear of being a widow? I could turn it off on my daily Dexter walks. Charlie's worry that SCAD was like an assassin boarding a bus to kill him? He could release that fear under the sixty-foot oaks with Dexter, his divine guard. We were each learning to be held by something much bigger.

Author and child-development researcher, L. R. Knost wrote:

When life feels too big to handle, go outside.
Everything looks smaller when you are standing under the sky.

Discovering new freedoms outside, Charlie was finding a way to cure his soul. Walking circles in my sacred park, I was remembering what a revelation it was just to be alive. Loving a dog so full of exuberance and purpose, we were each finding our way back to what brought us simple joys. Awakening outside under an endless sky, we were reminded daily of the much bigger world and life's much bigger plan.

8

LEARNING

THE SHIFT FROM CHRONOS TIME
TO KAIROS TIME

As Reverend Artress suggested in her labyrinth research, I had been releasing old ideas, seeking new ways of living, and trying to concede how little we control in this life. I had spent the first half of my life setting goals, believing in the life plans I had carefully constructed only to learn in the second half of my life that we really aren't in charge. We will continually need to recalculate and readjust when things don't go as planned.

With my newfound daily practice of musical meditative walking, I was starting to feel a peace that had eluded me since Charlie was first diagnosed. I no longer felt that I was on high alert, waiting for the next emergency room visit, and I was beginning to believe our toughest life lessons were over. I didn't understand we were not yet halfway through these major life detours, and I was going to need to recalibrate what I thought to be true.

It had been three years since Charlie's heart attack. Three years of careful, watchful, living hoping not to disturb Charlie's fragile arteries. In her research at Mayo Clinic, Dr. Sharonne Hayes had noted that patients who made it three years without another artery tear had a reasonably good prognosis. Charlie and I were feeling a new optimism that we might be able to return to normal and close this all-consuming medical-nightmare chapter in our lives.

In 2016, to celebrate being three years without another SCAD event as well as our three-decade anniversary, Charlie and I planned a Tuscany vacation we called our "Three for Thirty" trip. Three couples would be joining us on our bucket-list adventure. It was a blow-the-budget kind of excursion anticipating our final freedom from fearful living. We would leave on May 7, five days after Charlie's fifty-sixth birthday, so this vacation would be a triple celebration. As our departure date drew closer, Charlie's superstitious side began to kick in.

"What if we're just testing fate?" Charlie asked. "Maybe we should just thank our lucky stars that I'm still here and not risk an Italian emergency room visit."

I knew what he meant. I hadn't bothered trying to determine where the closest major medical center might be to our rented villa. How do you translate "cardiac catherization lab" in Italian? But I was feeling confident. Nothing had really happened in the three-year window so it was time to turn the page and begin living again. We decided to let Dr. Hayes weigh in and made an appointment at the Mayo Clinic two weeks before we would board the plane to Rome.

Being back in the Mayo medical bubble felt a little like Groundhog Day. We had been there before yet it seemed like a lifetime ago since we first heard the news that made Charlie feel like "an assassin had boarded a bus" to get him. We viewed this visit as our last trek to the Minnesota mecca and we were hopeful that Dr. Hayes would give Charlie the ultimate green light. If statistics showed that SCAD was less likely to happen again after three years, then it felt reasonable to believe that with this visit, we could close the book on bad news. We could finally put this terrifying medical calamity in the rearview mirror and never look back.

As we finished two days of testing and appointments, all signs were good. Tests showed the stents in Charlie's heart were working well and his EKG was unremarkable. In between appointments, we flipped through our upcoming Italian itinerary and dreamed about the wine waiting for us in two weeks' time. Our excitement continued to mount until our last consultation with Dr. Hayes. She knew we were headed out the door and not wanting to return. She knew we had a plane to catch back to Charlotte that afternoon as well as a flight to Italy in fourteen days. At the very end of our appointment, Dr. Hayes seemed to be summoning up courage to say what needed to be said. In past visits, she had always been very direct but this time, it felt as if she was avoiding eye contact with us.

"Your heart is looking so good, Charlie, that I hesitate to even bring this up," she said.

Her hands were folded calmly in her lap and her words were spoken softly but they still landed a blow.

"There are these spots on your lungs," she said.

She hated to even mention it but there were these spots. On his lungs. There were spots on Charlie's lungs.

"It's probably nothing," she said. "Sometimes, there can just be shadows that mean nothing."

But still, she wanted to run one more test to be sure.

Dr. Hayes waited patiently while Charlie and I fought about this news. Charlie was finished with being poked and prodded. He was only interested in his cardiac problem. If his heart and arteries were all fine, that's all he needed to know. Our flight back to Charlotte left in a few hours and Charlie was already mentally aboard, ready to celebrate in Italy. But I wanted Charlie to agree to the test. Dr. Hayes had already lined up an appointment to take a closer at Charlie's lungs, which meant she really didn't believe it was nothing. Dr. Hayes thought it was something.

"If we stay, we will miss our flight home," Charlie argued. "We can check it out in Charlotte with Dr. Jane when we get back from Italy."

"That is why we come to a place like Mayo," I insisted. "The best doctors. The best diagnostics. Immediate answers. Let's just do it now while we are here."

Dr. Hayes didn't want to get in the middle of our marital discourse, so she waited patiently for our feud to come to a conclusion. I won. Charlie went through with the test but he stewed on the long drive back to the Minneapolis airport for the flight we were now about to miss. As we left her office, Dr. Hayes assured us she would get the results immediately and email us the all clear.

In the rental car lot and throughout the airport security, Charlie checked his phone for confirmation from Dr. Hayes that "the spots" were nothing. As we boarded the plane, there was still no message from her. Perhaps the results were just taking longer on a busy Thursday. As our plane took off, there was still no word. Throughout the two-hour-and-forty-five-minute flight back to Charlotte, Charlie kept checking and refreshing his email with the onboard Wi-Fi. Just as the flight attendant announced that devices must be powered down for arrival into Charlotte, the email finally came through from Dr. Hayes.

I am so sorry it has taken so long to get back to you but I wanted to be sure. Could you come back in a week? We need to do a lung biopsy.

Apparently, the spots on Charlie's lungs were something. Dr. Hayes thought it might be a new condition unrelated to SCAD. Charlie and I read the email over and over wanting it to read differently.

All our hopes for a return to normal living. All our plans for celebration. All our intentions to turn the page on medical uncertainty. Now, we were not only panicked about Charlie's heart, we needed to worry about his lungs as well. Dr. Hayes's email told us there were several theories about what the spots could be, but a definitive diagnosis required further testing.

Ten days later on May 1, we boarded the plane back to Rochester. The next day would not only be the scheduled biopsy, it was Charlie's fifty-sixth birthday. Even though we were 1,100 miles from our home in Charlotte, everything in Rochester, Minnesota, was starting to feel eerily familiar. We checked into the same hotel. We ate at the same restaurant. We ordered and we didn't eat the same meal. This visit we wouldn't be in the main buildings filled will light and art. The surgery would take place about a mile away in a building that felt much less hopeful than the main campus.

The St. Mary's complex was still part of Mayo but a much older building with multiple newer additions. Inside the maze of hallways were 1,200 beds and 55 operating rooms for cutting-edge specialties like computer-assisted neurosurgery and heart transplants. Charlie's lung biopsy would be simple compared to other procedures but it felt dire to us. A heart problem as well as a lung problem? Arguably two of the most vital organs in his body were both somehow compromised.

I don't remember exactly what Charlie and I talked about those ten days between not knowing and knowing. I don't remember waiting in a waiting room or even how long the procedure took. But I remember meeting Dr. Craig Daniels after the lung biopsy. He was younger than I imagined, maybe midforties, with a tall forehead, charcoal hair just beginning to fleck gray, and a straight white smile. He could not have been kinder when he shook our hands and sat comfortably on the edge of Charlie's bed in the recovery unit. He could not have been calmer when he told us that along with SCAD, Charlie also now had another rare condition called sarcoidosis.

Another rare condition. The spots on Charlie's lungs were tiny collections of inflammatory cells called 'granulomas' that can occur when the body's immune system is responding as if to an attack from an unknown substance.

As Dr. Daniels spoke, we were in complete shock just trying to absorb the new medical language associated with the lungs. We were well-versed in arteries and dissections but granulomas and immune systems? This was new territory. I heard Dr. Daniels saying something about the lungs of people who had been near the World Trade Center.

"Sarcoidosis is not common but we have seen it in first responders to the World Trade Center," Dr. Daniels said.

"Charlie's office in New York is two blocks from that site," I said. "He wasn't there on 9/11 but he was there the week after and most weeks since."

Maybe that could explain it. But really, how can you possibly explain how one formerly fit, healthy male inexplicably contracts two rare diseases in three years?

"It's possible," Dr. Daniels said about Charlie's proximity and repeated exposure to the 9/11 air. "We are not exactly sure what causes sarcoidosis. Some people seem to be genetically predisposed, and then, it becomes triggered by a bacterium, a virus, or maybe a contaminant in the air experienced by the 9/11 responders."

"What's the cure?" asked Charlie jumping straight to the endgame. "How do I get rid of it?"

"There is no cure," Dr. Daniels said. "But we can manage symptoms."

Another incurable rare disease.

We would learn that symptoms depend on which organs are affected and that was the really crushing news. Sarcoidosis is not just limited to lungs. It can invade a patient's other organs most notably eyes, kidneys, and heart. Dr. Daniels gently let us know we would now need to check Charlie's other organs for signs of sarcoidosis before we could leave Rochester. The efficiencies of Mayo Clinic meant all those tests could be scheduled right away and we would have fast answers. Even if they weren't the answers we wanted to know.

Charlie and I sat across from each other at our favorite Italian restaurant in Rochester. We had now spent so much time there we had a favorite restaurant. We were supposed to be celebrating Charlie's birthday but there was a bottle of wine and plates of food we weren't interested in finishing. It was difficult to imagine how we had arrived here in only three years' time. From a man who jumped out of helicopters into fresh powder at 10,000 feet to a guy who had not one, but two rare diseases in the same body—each potentially fatal. Before we left the clinic, I asked Dr. Daniels about that probability. Along with being a world-class pulmonologist, Dr. Daniels supervised the Mayo Emergency Department and he had two decades of experience with medial anomalies.

"How is it possible that Charlie could have not one, but *two* rare diseases?" I asked.

"I can't explain that," he said.

I tried asking another way. "Do you know any other patient who has both SCAD and sarcoidosis in the same body?"

Dr. Craig Daniels, medical expert and emergency room warrior, shook his head without saying a word.

Miraculously, we would leave Rochester with the relatively good news that sarcoidosis was currently only present in Charlie's lungs. His eyes, kidneys, and even his heart, seemed to be unaffected—for now. All of Charlie's organs would now need to be monitored. There would be more appointments.

After endless debates and conferences with Dr. Jane and Dr. Hayes, we unpacked from Minnesota and repacked for Tuscany as planned. It was still our thirtieth wedding anniversary. It was still good news that Charlie was three years past his initial SCAD. It was still a miracle that he had lived to see his fifty-sixth birthday. We were committed to having a great time with great friends. But upon leaving for Italy, we were still so fearful.

"Did you see what gate we are leaving from?" Charlie asked in the Charlotte airport headed to Rome.

"I did," I said. "Thirteen."

As I turned to look at him, Charlie appeared stricken. From the past week of a lung biopsy to the past three years of cardiac catastrophe, all of it was etched on Charlie's face. I tried to think of something that could ease his terror of dying.

"Even if we were leaving from gate 13 on May 13 on flight 1313 sitting in row 13, it wouldn't mean you were going to die," I said. "None of those things would matter. If it's going to happen, it is going to happen." We hugged tightly in the lounge, and then we boarded the plane.

What I remember most about that trip is that we were not careful. Instead, we were carefree for the first time in three years which, given our recent news of sarcoidosis, was somewhat of a paradox. We had been so cautious for three years about everything. About being within one hour of a cardiac catherization lab. About Charlie's exercise. About how many pounds he lifted. About our bank account that Charlie was trying so hard to stockpile so that he could feel he had made enough for us in case he died.

But those seven days in Italy? Somehow, we were completely carefree. We splurged in restaurants. We stayed up late laughing and dancing with our friends. We drank wine every day at lunch and dinner and we were convinced it was not just the scenery that made it the best wine we had ever tasted. We let go. We lived in the moment.

It was a seven-day stretch of fully living and appreciating each amazing day. From the views of the hills of Montepulciano to the comforting homemade Italian pasta, it all seemed to be the best food in the best place we had ever been.

During every one of those moments, I am sure Charlie might have been at risk. At any time, I am sure it is possible Charlie could have needed an ambulance or he could have needed to pull out the laminated card he carried with a detailed description of his SCAD information written in English, which would have been no help to an Italian ER doctor. I am sure in a Milan hospital, we would have not been able to find the translation for sarcoidosis or Spontaneous Coronary Artery Dissection. But in that week, surrounded by the best of friends with the best of food, I had not felt that safe or that joyful in three years. I doubt Dr. Jane or Dr. Hayes or Dr. Daniels could have prescribed anything better.

When we were in the midst of all our Tuscan adventures, I could not have explained how we forgot all that was happening and just celebrated life. How we shifted our perspective from minute-by-minute worry to moment-by-moment joy. At first, I thought maybe it was just the full-bodied wine and the enchantment of ancient hilltop towns. And then later, I thought maybe it was the safety of being gathered with our best friends. Just like being a part of Steve's band of love surrounding his home was so uplifting, despite the fact that our friend was dying.

Looking back, I believe those days in Italy showed me that it was possible to live time differently. It was years after our Italian escape when I read this passage written by Sue Monk Kidd in *When the Heart Waits: Spiritual Direction for Life's Sacred Questions*:

There are two words for time in the Bible: Chronos and Kairos. When Chronos dominates, we live by time. Life is experienced as chronology, as one thing happening after another. This is a linear way of thinking about time, with the relentless cadence of tick-tock, tick-tock. The sound takes up residence in us. . . . When Kairos dominates, we live in time, in the deep dot. Life is experienced as opportunity. Kairos is full time, real time. It requires dwelling in the moment so completely, that the possibility of life opens up to us.

Over the past three years, Charlie and I had been living every day of our lives in medical trauma and Chronos time. In the "relentless cadence" of fear that each minute might be Charlie's last. And even though we had been granted a new chance at this life together when he survived his heart attack three years before, we were still living full of regret for what we lost instead of full of gratitude for what we gained.

Boarding the plane to Italy with fresh fears of a new lung diagnosis piled on top of cardiac worries, I could not have imagined being able to escape the new anxiety. I am sure every moment of the flight to Rome, I thought only of Charlie dying. But somewhere in the Tuscan hillside, surrounded by friends and sunsets and the history of all that had happened there in the hundreds of years before we ever arrived as tourists, Charlie and I forgot all about the potential of dying from SCAD and sarcoidosis. We remembered what a gift it is just to be alive. We savored that thought. We lived our days in Kairos time.

It is, of course, easy to live well and joyously on vacation. The trick is developing joy, reverence, and gratitude for each day without leaving home. No matter how many more days we had together, Charlie and I needed to find a way to shift our focus from minute-by-minute worry to moment-by-moment joy. I could only tolerate living with rare disease if I made a full-life switch from Chronos time to Kairos time.

RECEIVING

No intervention and no interventionist can "cure" our grief. And we are not broken—we are brokenhearted. Grief is not a medical disorder to be cured. Grief is not a spiritual crisis to be resolved. Grief is not a social woe to be addressed. Grief is, simply, a matter of the heart—to be felt.

JOANNE CACCIATORE, PHD,
Bearing the Unbearable: Love, Loss, and the Heartbreaking Path of Grief

9

GROUNDING

WE MAKE THE WAY
BY WALKING

After Italy, I felt I was fully releasing control, understanding exactly how much was uncontrollable in my daily life. Remembering my labyrinth walk, it was as if the past three years I had been winding my way toward the center rosette of life where I hoped to be receiving new knowledge and understanding. While I was unable to see my destination, I was learning to trust the path before me and tolerate the radical uncertainty in which we continued to live.

My daily walking practice had already taught me how grounded I felt when I was under the trees feeling my problems were smaller under big skies. But it was walking 100 kilometers of an ancient sacred path that truly helped me discover to trust each step even when I could not see the road before me.

In 2010, I watched a film called *The Way* and left the theater mesmerized. Throughout the movie, I kept thinking, "Is this a real place? How have I never heard of this?" *The Way* is a feature film written and

directed by Emilio Estevez and it stars his father, Martin Sheen. While
the film is a fictional account of one man's travels, it tells the true story
of the famous pilgrimage in Spain called the "Camino de Santiago."
In English, the path's name translates to "The Way of St. James." This
famous 500-mile journey has been traveled by millions of "pilgrims"
since the Middle Ages. Although there are many across Europe, all
roads lead to the cathedral known as the "Santiago de Compostela" in
Galicia, Spain, where the remains of the apostle James are buried.

The movie, *The Way*, captures the spirit of the Camino by depicting
all those who walk the ancient path seeking spiritual enlightenment.
Some after divorce. Some after death. Some just trying to find a simpler way to live in an increasingly hectic modern world. After seeing
the movie, I went home and Googled all about the Camino, vowing
that someday I would make that same walk. But then life got busy,
Charlie got sick, and I forgot all about my promise. It wasn't until 2016
when my friend, Anne Stolz, asked me to join her on a trip to walk the
Camino that I renewed my vow. I committed to the trip with Anne,
and, eventually, fourteen friends would join us for the Spanish experience.

Imagining the adventure ahead, I was eager to acquire my blisters
and accrue tales of how I had survived the Camino. I wanted to earn
my 'stamps' on my Pilgrim Passport. This official Camino credential
(Credencia del Peregrino) was historically a scallop seashell. Ancient pilgrims pulled a shell from the ocean and had it validated in each town
they passed through on their way to the famous sanctuary, Santiago de
Compostela. It was even legend that "peregrinos" (Spanish for "spiritual
pilgrims") could one day show this 'passport' to St. Peter at the gates of
heaven to 'prove' they had earned entrance through a lifetime of pious
living.

After over a year of planning and walking hundreds of training
miles, our group arrived in Burgos, Spain, in September 2016. Some of

us were family, others were friends, so our meeting felt like a reunion even though some of us had never met. As we gathered in our hotel for our initial meeting with guides, Patricia and David, our excitement was high and our chatter was loud.

As we convened around a long wooden banquet table, Patricia welcomed us to our coming spiritual adventure. After describing our route and the trip details, she turned the questions to us. Since embarking on this path is traditionally a holy endeavor, Patricia asked each of us to share with the group our reasons for walking.

As we listened to each other's stories, I realized I wasn't really sure why I had come. Initially, I had been drawn to this path because of the movie, but really, I had long felt a divine whisper around this trip. Every time I heard the word "Camino," I also heard a small inner voice encouraging, "*Yes, that!*" When Anne asked me to sign on, I had the whisper as a shout I could not ignore: "*Do it!*"

Aside from the promise of adventure, I wasn't sure why I had heard that whisper so loudly. At the time, I believed the "test" of walking so many miles over so many days would teach me something. Although I understood we were not completing the full 500 miles, I still expected our trip to be a physical challenge until Patricia delivered a curveball.

In heavily accented English, Patricia informed us, "In all, we will be walking 100 kilometers and tomorrow is a light day—about four miles."

Four miles? What?

For months, I had trained expecting daily ten-mile hikes, but Patricia had just said *kilometers,* not *miles.* Doing the new math, I realized we would only be walking 62 miles in total—a little over half of what I imagined. Patricia was outlining a far-less-intense journey. Not only would we travel less than eight miles a day, but a van would pick us up at designated spots to whisk us to our next inn.

Hardly the arduous adventure I had imagined with blisters and barriers to overcome.

We were fourteen, mostly Type A, American tourists absorbing all this. Those of us who were hoping for more rigor and who were accustomed to more control in our travel, pressed Patricia.

"But we could walk more miles a day if we want to, right?"

Patricia shook her head, "No."

Maybe there was a language barrier.

"Well, we could walk past the van sometimes and they could come back to get us, right?"

Patricia shook her head, "No."

Not only was Patricia repeatedly telling us *No*, but she also looked completely confused that we would even suggest changing her itinerary. Patricia had walked the Camino dozens of times and she assured us that this was not only the best route, but it was also the best way to experience it.

As our meeting dispersed, we still couldn't let go. "I am sure we can walk more," Anne muttered to me.

"We can run ahead and then double back to log more miles!" I told her.

I texted Charlie to tell him about the change of plans, but with the six-hour time difference, he was undoubtedly asleep and didn't answer. For a moment, my familiar panic rose, wondering if he was really sleeping at 3:00 a.m. or if something had happened while I wasn't there. Maybe that was one of the reasons I had come to Spain. After more than three years of constant concern, I knew I subconsciously believed Charlie's health and well-being was my job—not the doctors. He so often told people, "Kathy is my guardian angel. If she had let me take a nap that day, I wouldn't be here." Maybe part of this Camino trip was to show me a way to trust that Charlie could survive without me.

The next morning, we gathered to walk as an excited pack of new and old friends in our matching "Camino 2016" shirts. We came together as friends, cousins, sisters, mothers, and empty nesters, still unsure what we had gotten ourselves into. We all had day backpacks with water, bandanas, extra layers, socks, Band-Aids, walking sticks—clearly overprepared for what we would begin calling our "Princess Pilgrimage."

Our journey began at the Burgos Cathedral, declared a World Heritage site for the classic Gothic architecture and thirteenth-century craftsmanship, which had taken almost three hundred years to complete. Our historical guide, David, directed our attention to a huge piece of limestone above the entrance. Carved into the stone were the twelve apostles, each appearing to be reading—except for St. James. Instead of looking at his pages, this apostle was pointing to the large scallop shell carved on the front cover. He was pointing to this iconic symbol of the Way of St. James—the Camino de Santiago.

"You see?" David said. He spoke in an animated fashion with expansive hand gestures and an abiding enthusiasm for this journey I was only beginning to understand. "He is saying, 'Close your books! The Way is out here!'"

It was a powerful picture to carve into stone hundreds of years ago, this idea that studying religion and reading about faith could only take you so far. To truly develop faith, James suggested we must actually experience life. As I left the Burgos Cathedral to walk our first four miles of the trek, I kept turning this idea over in my head. In my everyday life, I had been reading so much about faith, but was I really believing anything?

Remembering the stone carving and St. James's insistence that "the way" is discovered on the road itself, I reset my intention for the week. I readjusted from a primary goal of logging miles to a new goal of enjoying each moment. I wanted to be fully present on this sacred road that for hundreds of years had been teaching its followers. And to understand that all those on this journey created a community which was in itself a communion.

Maybe all along, my pilgrimage was not supposed to be about blisters. Maybe it was supposed to be about bliss. Maybe the reason I had come to Spain was to experience the pure joy of being alive with no other mission than to be awed by the holiness of our human journey.

Over the next seven days, our group established a rhythm. With our jet lag behind us, we filled our Camelpacks with water and were ready to walk well before 8:00 a.m. Each morning, it was restorative to have no other purpose for the day except to wake up and put one foot in front of the other. I realized I couldn't remember a morning in the past ten years—the past twenty years—where I didn't have something I *needed* to do. When was the last time I woke up and asked myself, "What do I *want* to do?"

Not what I *had* to do. Not what I was *required* of me to do. What I *wanted* to do.

So much of my past ten years had been spent in a frenzy of doing. Housing the homeless. Raising four children. Researching rare disease. It was a completely new experience for me to have no idea what I was going to do or what I would see that day. Each morning, I discovered I loved waking in unexpected wonder.

Those days on the Camino—just waking up, allowing the road to reveal itself, letting someone else be the guide—were a revelation. I loved hiking through woods without a map, not worrying where the path might take me. Coming around a corner, I might be surprised by a spectacular field of sunflowers or an unexpected grove of shade. Every mealtime, we arrived in a different cobblestone village where, because of our guides, the innkeeper had been expecting us. Steaming bowls of soup, baskets of fresh bread, platters of Ibérico ham and Manchego cheese magically appeared on a long table set for our arrival. Each night, after much conversation under stars I had not noticed in years, I drifted to sleep thinking about the balance I needed to find in my life. Some resting between running. Some breathing along with the achieving.

As I listened to David explaining each sacred cathedral or artifact, for the first time in my life I was not dismissing religious significance, but instead contemplating the meaning for myself. My complicated history with my own faith had left me too dismissive of religion. As I walked along the road so many thousands of travelers had walked before me seeking enlightenment or atonement, it occurred to me how I had abandoned all theology in my teenage rebellion from religion. Because I could not find a faith that fit between agnosticism and fundamentalism, I had given up on God too soon. That seemed to be the root cause of the spiritual homelessness I constantly wrestled with and all my reading was only one way to find my way home. This pilgrimage was starting to feel like a fast track to finding a faith I could believe in.

One afternoon as we approached the small mountain town of Villafranca del Bierzo, David had us all gather along a rustic stone wall in front of a cathedral. While it was a small chapel in comparison to others we had toured, this church was huge relative to the tiny village where it was built.

"This is 'la pequeña Compostela,'" David said with his signature grin. "The little Compostela."

This twelfth-century cathedral had become famous along the Camino for travelers unable to continue their journey all the way to

Santiago. Like the famous cathedral that was our destination, this smaller version was built with a "Puerta del Perdón," which translated to a "Door of Forgiveness." David explained that pilgrims pass through this doorway seeking atonement and the promise of new life. The symbolic crossing of this threshold represents leaving this world and embracing the grace in the kingdom of God.

After David's explanation, it sounded like a powerful rite of passage that I wanted to experience. Except, today, the door was closed.

"The door is only open at certain times," David told us. Since 1470, the Catholic Church decreed that the doors of forgiveness here, as well as in Santiago, are only open during "Holy Years."

As David explained all this, I was filled with regret. I desperately wanted to walk through that door. It felt like a holy threshold through which I must pass. So many doorways I had been pushed through unwillingly—the SCAD Door, the Rare Disease Door, the Sarcoidosis Door. I wanted to choose this threshold and direct my own crossing.

As others rested along the rock wall outside the Little Compostela for a water break, I pressed closer to the large wooden doors, feeling the coolness offered by the stone shadow of the cathedral. I pressed my back against the cool, stone walls and slid to the ground with my eyes closed. Resting against the small cathedral walls, I allowed myself to feel supported and held. Like the trees in my favorite park back home, I rested in the shade, pausing to reflect.

If the doors magically opened and I could walk through, what would I ask for?

With my eyes still pressed shut, I imagined myself passing through the massive wooden Doors of Forgiveness and nestling into a pew. For years, I imagined I was wandering aimlessly through my life when all the while, I was becoming exactly who I needed to be. I wanted forgiveness for so many things. To forgive myself for time lost in pursuit of wrong paths. To forgive myself for waiting for so long to look for my life. To release the last three years wasted living in fear instead of faith. For worrying about all I thought I had lost instead of being in awe of all I had found.

Before I had left for this pilgrimage, it felt as if everything about my life was shaking and shifting. Would Charlie live? When would the next ambulance ride whisk him away? How would I ever live on this earth without my soul mate, my Goose, beside me? But during those eight days walking an ancient road, I had found a way to ground myself. A way to connect to a larger spiritual tradition. A way to walk my way toward faith.

My goal had been to conquer the Camino, imagining the only reason to walk would simply be the accomplishment of 100 miles logged. Instead, I had found a new way of being in communion with a community of women I would never be able to replace. I had found a reverence for religion that had eluded me my whole life. I might return to walk this Way again, but I could never repeat it as with these women. My first trip along the ancient Spanish road would always be its own special kind of holy.

When I embarked upon my Camino pilgrimage, I did not understand what a powerful experience it would be in my life both during the trip and long after. In experiencing a pilgrimage, a traveler brings home far more than exotic photos and happy memories. Best-selling author and host of the PBS series, *Sacred Journeys*, Bruce Feiler, writes and researches about sacred travel. In 2014, he went on six famous pilgrimages to understand this ancient practice that has modern day significance. He published an article about his thoughts in a *New York Times* article, "The

New Allure of Sacred Journeys." Feiler asserted that Americans were joining the spiritual travel boom in growing numbers at the same time regular church attendance is declining for good reason:

> *It's that feeling of taking control over one's life that most affected the pilgrims I met. So much of religion as it's been practiced for centuries has been largely passive. People receive a faith from their parents; they are herded into institutions they have no role in choosing; they spend much of their spiritual lives sitting inactively in buildings being lectured at from on high.*
>
> *A pilgrimage reverses all of that. At its core, it's a gesture of action. In a world in which more and more things are artificial and ephemeral, a sacred journey gives the pilgrim the chance to experience something both physical and real. And it provides seekers with an opportunity they may never have had: to confront their doubts and decide for themselves what they really believe.*

Like the estimated 330 million people who travel annually as part of a pilgrimage, the questions I pondered walking the Camino began to shape what I believe. Among the many lessons I brought home, this quote by Spanish poet, Antonio Machado, remains my favorite:

> **Caminante, no hay camino, se hace camino al andar.**
> *Traveler, there is no way. You make the way by walking.*

Like my brief morning experience in the Sacred Garden at the church labyrinth, the Camino was an extended lesson in trusting the life path in front of me. As much as I want to set a course, make a plan, attain a goal, life is, in fact, unchartable. Maybe that would be the strongest ingredient yet I had found for mixing my own recipe for the gold epoxy that I could use to fix all that felt broken. My golden glue begins to be mixed, by understanding that there is no sure plan that I can use to guide my life and no map that guides me to absolute certainty. It is about taking the next right step, and then the next. Choosing a destination but understanding there will be unexpected detours and some of them, far better than your intended landing place.

There is no one way. You make the way by walking.

10

SPIRALING

THE DISCOVERY OF HOW
STRONG WE CAN BECOME

Returning from the Camino, I felt completely transformed. With my feet firmly grounded in a new understanding of seeing God, I believed I was prepared for anything. In my naivete, I thought my journey was complete. I had walked a long road both physically and metaphorically. I had Released old ways of thinking, Received new knowledge, and Returned to my world full of my new wisdom for resiliency. What I didn't yet understand, is that just like walking a labyrinth, figuring out life is never merely a one-time lesson. We must keep spiraling toward God on this inner journey and with each passage we gain new knowledge.

The past four years living with SCAD and sarcoidosis were like being on a plane where the pilot announced for all the passengers to prepare for a crash landing. I had been holding my knees and my breath for so long that my panic had finally subsided and I had stopped believing there was actually ever going to be a crash. Until the morning of January 2, 2017, when I got the call from Charlie.

"Kathy, can you meet me at the ER?"

That was not what I was expecting Charlie to say when I picked up my phone. I was past the days of constantly checking my phone screen expecting to be summoned to an emergency room. It seemed I had even forgotten that we were ever even in danger.

Everything had been going so well. Just two nights before, our family had attended a huge New Year's party with all of our daughters and we had danced past midnight. Even months later, people would say to me, "I was so surprised to hear what happened to Charlie after watching him dance with your girls that night."

When I finally found Charlie in the emergency room, he was definitely not dancing. As I pulled back the thin curtain screen, Charlie made an attempt to smile at me, but I could see he was frightened. Most concerning, his hands were crossed above his chest clutching his biceps. His posture of pain was eerily similar to almost four years before when he had collapsed on the hotel bed in Massachusetts.

"I went to see Dr. Jane this morning on the way to work to ask her about my arms," he said. "She thought I should come to the emergency room."

Over the past few years, Charlie had experienced all types of chest pains, pricks, and spasms. I think this is the most difficult part for patients who have lived through cardiac trauma. How do you decide which pains to pay attention to? Which ones are normal and which ones catastrophic? It can drive you crazy with worry wondering if you are overreacting or if you truly are at risk.

As we waited in the ER for preliminary test results, our emergency room technician told us something I still remember.

"It's the fifties that will kill you," he said, connecting Charlie to the EKG monitor. "Everyone in their fifties imagines they are so healthy. They ignore signs and think they are fine. I would rather you come in nine times and I send you home nine times. It is the tenth one you ignore—that's the one that will kill you."

Although these words were a jolt of reality, I appreciated the tech's honesty because he was making Charlie feel as if he was not overreacting. But was he really telling us he thought this was Charlie's "tenth time"? Was this going to be the one that would actually kill him? As we waited for test results, we worried. Whatever this was, Charlie was not in a crisis situation like our ambulance ride in Massachusetts, but clearly, it wasn't normal either.

"I don't feel that bad," Charlie assured the girls as we called each one with the news. "I am sure I will be home tomorrow."

Charlie didn't come home the next day or the day after that. Cardiologists determined that the two stents, only four years old, were failing. Opinions varied, however, on what exactly could be done. How could they operate or repair arteries that were as fragile as Charlie's? Complicating the already difficult procedure, doctors had to consider Charlie's weakened lungs due to the newly discovered sarcoidosis.

After three days, we finally prepared to leave the hospital but it wasn't to go home. It was to board an air ambulance to Mayo Clinic to seek the expertise of Dr. Hayes and Dr. Craig who might understand what to do for their doubly difficult patient. Their opinion shocked us.

"Open-heart surgery," they each said in separate consultations. "We recommend you have open-heart surgery."

Open. Heart. Surgery. We had not even known this was on the medical menu for us to consider. Charlie was only fifty-six years old.

Charlie's stents were failing years too soon. *Restenosis* they called it. Even though the stents Dr. Ali used were state-of-the-art devices designed to last a decade or more, Charlie's were, in fact, no longer working. Charlie's arm pain was caused by the blood flow once again being restricted in his heart as his artery struggled to remain open. Unlike his heart attack, however, there was not a dissection. This time there was a slow, potentially fatal, closing of his artery.

The surgeon who came to talk with us confidently recommended the best course of action would be to create a new cardiac pathway. Essentially, the surgeon planned to reroute the blood flow in his heart. The failing stents could not be removed but this new blood highway would bypass the problem. The recovery would be four to six months, but the solution would be lasting—at least for that one pathway in Charlie's heart. There would still be no guarantee for all the other arteries throughout his body which could dissect at any time.

"We can do the surgery day after tomorrow on Monday," the surgeon told us.

Once again with only twenty-four-hour notice, each of our four daughters put their lives on hold and gathered around their dad, this time in Minnesota, not Massachusetts. Just like in 2013, unknown planes, trains, and automobiles enabled Lauren, Kailey, Emma, and Maddie to appear in an angelic array around Charlie on the Sunday morning before his surgery. It had only been a week since we gathered in a New Year's dance circle, and now we gathered together in a prayer circle.

Unlike 2013 when the girls arrived knowing Charlie's life had already been saved, this time had no idea what would happen. We weren't celebrating the miracle of making it through a sudden heart attack and life-saving catherization. We were at the top of a cardiac cliff, terrified of the sheer drop below us. Would the surgery work? Could this surgeon successfully reroute the blood flow of arteries that spontaneously dissected? How would Charlie's sarcoidosis condition with weakened lung capacity complicate general anesthesia for the predicted eight-hour procedure?

There would be hours and hours to ponder those questions as we waited. And waited. By dinnertime, we had already been on high alert for twelve hours, but really, the tension had started in Charlotte over a week before with the call to meet Charlie in the emergency room.

Finally at 9:00 p.m., a nurse led me, Lauren, Kailey, Emma and Maddie to a small room designed for three people. We huddled in the nine-foot cubicle sharing chairs and bumping knees until the surgeon arrived with his blue surgical cap in hand. Although he was only in his thirties or forties, he had thick, graying hair matted from his cap and long day's work. He seemed surprised that there were so many of us pressed into the room waiting for him.

"I am sorry that took so long," he apologized.

We held our collective breaths.

"He's doing well," he said with a smile. "He did really well."

The five us collapsed in relief. We hugged—individually and then group hugged—and hugged again. We held tight our circle of five certain that we would return to six. Charlie was still in recovery but the surgeon told us to get some dinner because it would be a few hours before Charlie woke up from anesthesia.

As the girls and I gathered in a restaurant across the street from the hospital, the waitress didn't know what to make of us. A mom and four daughters celebrating something on a Monday night in Minnesota. It wasn't a birthday but it felt like a new day, a new beginning for Charlie with a new artery. We ordered a bottle of wine and raised our glasses, giddy with relief that Charlie would be okay. *We would all be okay.*

It was almost 11:30 p.m. when the ICU nurse texted that Charlie was finally waking up. Rushing to pay the bill, we hurried through the snow to see Charlie and I truly thought I was prepared. But there is nothing that prepares you to see the fifty-six-year-old man you love, who once willingly, fearlessly, flung himself out of helicopters, now surrounded by machines, swallowed in tubing, and clinging to life. Nothing prepared me for that. In the same intake of breath, I wanted to cry that Charlie was alive and sob that he looked all but dead.

I remember moving as if in slow motion to touch Charlie's hand and hoping he might open his eyes to give me some sign of the "Goose" I so loved. But he was still between worlds. Between this one pumped full of anesthesia and the next one full of bright white light. He was pale. He was lying in bed. He was alive. But he was so not Charlie.

In that moment at his hospital bedside, I realized that surviving the surgery and living were not the same. Charlie still had so far to go. To be that guy who jumped out of helicopters or even the guy who could walk around the block. At that moment, I wondered for the first time, if Charlie would ever make it back, truly all the way back, to anything he loved. While the girls held hands and whispered to their semiconscious dad, I backed slowly out of the room.

In the hallway, I pressed my spine against the hospital wall and collapsed in exhaustion. The past week of living in constant emergency had been seven days of being on high alert. From the emergency room to the air ambulance to the first time doctors mentioned "open-heart surgery," to this moment.

But really, it had been four years of high alert. Of wondering every moment if Charlie's arteries were intact. Of living with nightmares of slow leaks or big bursts. Of imagining heart attacks or strokes or clots or even lung spots that could threaten Charlie's life and being terrified that at any moment he could die. Suddenly, I was so tired—so bone tired. Every cell in my body felt like it had been fighting, trying to control, feeling personally responsible as Charlie's "guardian angel" for making sure he stayed alive. And now, I had nothing left.

I had hoped this surgery would be what we needed to find peace and resume living a normal life. But seeing Charlie and realizing how far we still had to go, I was completely depleted. This wasn't just a tree well we had fallen into. This was a medical avalanche with a deep, heavy snow of complications that was about to smother any sign of life remaining in either of us. I didn't know who could possibly dig us out or if we would still be breathing when they found us. I felt buried alive.

Even after four years, I never saw it coming. I didn't know I could spiral deeper and deeper and still survive. I didn't know my biggest lesson was still to learn. And I didn't yet understand that feeling of aloneness was connecting me to something so much bigger.

In *Untamed*, Glennon Doyle Melton writes about visiting her dying grandmother:

Somehow I am here with everyone who has ever lived and ever loved and ever lost. I have entered the place I thought was death and it has turned out to be life itself. I entered this ache alone but inside it I have found everyone. In surrendering to the ache of loneliness I have discovered unloneliness. Right here. Inside the ache with everyone who has ever welcomed a child or held the hand of a dying grandmother, or said goodbye to a great love. I am here with all of them. . . . Inside, the ache is the we. We can do hard things like be alive and love deep and lose it all because we do these things alongside everyone who has ever walked the earth with her eyes, arms, and heart wide open.

When we are on our last leg, it doesn't matter how many times we are knocked down—only that we get up again. As Dr. Rachel Naomi Remen advised, "What happens next is very, very important."

There is a Japanese proverb adopted from a Buddhist teaching, "Seven times down. Eight up." I felt I had fallen down seven times and getting up this eighth time, my knees were definitely buckling. There are moments that might push each of us to our breaking point. An accident that damaged a heart more than a vehicle. An experimental treatment that didn't work. A miscarriage of a child already dearly loved.

When they happen we are stunned. We didn't know we would have to face such difficulties. We didn't know we would have to keep getting up. We didn't know we would have to do so many hard things. But as we spiral down each time, if we allow the experience to move us a little closer to discovering what we believe, we learn how strong we truly can become.

11

REVIVING

EACH DAY IS
A HOLY PLACE

After witnessing Charlie at his weakest, I found my strength. As a mother and wife, I couldn't choose to quit. There are always people counting on us to keep waking up even when we don't want to. The dog still needs to be fed. Dinner still needs to be made. Work still needs us to check our inbox.

Sarah Bessey, author of *Miracles and Other Reasonable Things*, endured years of physical suffering after a car accident left her with broken bones and at times, a broken spirit. Bessey writes:

No one ever told us how much courage it takes to have a broken-heart, did they? No one told us how brave we would have to be to simply carry on. And yet here you are. I pray for courage to rise up in you so that you can get up out of bed for another day and do what you need to do to carry on.

Sometimes even the most mundane tasks can become a lifeline to help us carry on. Going through the motions—brushing teeth, washing dishes, folding clothes—can be the routine that helps us find our rhythm again. We remember we can do hard things.

After Charlie's open-heart surgery, I was finding my rhythm in our hospital routine. Each day the same: wake up, meet with doctors, sit with Charlie, go to sleep, repeat. Kailey, Emma, and Maddie had all hugged their dad goodbye, returned to their respective jobs and colleges relieved to know the worst was behind us. Since Lauren was in graduate school and classes had not resumed, she planned to stay the week with me in Minnesota.

Grateful for her company, I had settled into a schedule with Lauren for caring for our patient, Charlie. Usually, I would wake up, cross the icy sludge in the street from hotel to hospital to be first to Charlie's bedside for the early-morning doctor rounds. Lauren would arrive late morning to sit beside Charlie, and I would leave to exercise in the hotel gym. The three of us would have lunch together and then we would rotate afternoon shifts until hospital visiting hours were over.

By three days post-surgery, Charlie had slowly been coming back to life. One by one, tubes were removed and he only had two lines connecting him to outside forces: an IV and a heart monitor. An eleven-inch opening on his chest was closing remarkably fast due to advanced wound-healing strips that were miraculously sealing Charlie's sternum. His main daily activity was trying to walk just a few steps around the halls. Charlie was determined to defy expectations by recovering in only eight weeks instead of the predicted six months. Despite his best efforts, however, Charlie's recovery wasn't progressing as quickly as he planned. The ten steps to the bathroom were an effort, and navigating the ten yards of hallway was a challenge that actually caused him to sweat.

It was dinnertime on his third day post-surgery and Charlie was finishing his meal, feeling a little celebratory after completing his first full lap of the cardiac ICU.

"You and Lauren get out of here tonight," Charlie said between bites of salad and chicken. "Go do something normal like have a good dinner in a restaurant."

I had to admit, that would be a nice change and it did feel like Charlie's recovery was beginning to accelerate. Lauren was in the hotel gym so I texted her the new plan for dining out. She replied with a flurry of enthusiastic emojis. As I checked my phone for new messages from friends and family, Charlie's night nurse came into the room with a young male resident.

"We are going to add a drug to help your heart rhythm," the nurse told Charlie as she reached for his IV pole.

While he had been recovering well, Charlie's heartbeat had not stabilized since surgery and this new medication was the potential solution. Charlie still had electrodes in his chest from the surgery and they snaked from under his hospital gown to the heart monitor which blinked silently by his bedside. The electric pulse from Charlie's heart registered as a bright-green line waving steadily in a series of ascending and descending humps on the EKG machine beside his bed. For the past twenty-four hours, we had been very focused on this wavy lifeline which had been slightly erratic. Cardiologists had been studying Charlie's rhythms and the goal was to smooth the line to a predictable pattern of even, healthy peaks and valleys.

Concentrating on my iPhone, I wasn't paying much attention as Charlie made small talk with his nurse. The male resident was administering the new medicine through Charlie's IV line and the nurse was fiddling with the dial on the heart monitor. Suddenly, Charlie's body jerked and I heard him say, "Don't do that again, I might pass out."

As I turned to look at Charlie, my world flipped upside down.

I remember seeing Charlie's eyes roll back in his head and his entire body lurch in a frightening, unnatural spasm. The nurse and the resident began rushing too fast in too small a space. Small beeps turned into loud alarms that morphed into sirens and exploded into overhead announcements. *Code Blue* it blared. *Code Blue.*

Suddenly, the room was filled with people. Too many people. Doctors, nurses, residents. A medical swarm. As if on cue, one nurse separated from this hive, grabbing my elbow to pull me through the doorway. We careened into another nurse who was trying to enter the room with what I learned later was a cardiac crash cart.

"What is happening?" I wailed.

"Cardiac arrest," she said softly. "Your husband is in cardiac arrest."

I didn't understand. *Charlie was fine. Everything had been fine.* How could Charlie be having another heart attack? It was like reliving the same horrible day all over again from four years ago.

Heart Attack? When did he have a heart attack?

Charlie was eating dinner and then, he was jerking and then, he wasn't there. But unlike 2013, this time, I knew. Some part of my brain knew because I had seen it. My mind just didn't allow me to process it. But I could not mistake what I saw right before the nurse pulled me from the room. Before she pushed me out the door, I had glimpsed at the monitor.

It had a flat green line.

Not the bright, healthy, verdant peaks. A grim, green, flat line. Like on the television shows when the camera does a closeup on the monitor to let you know that the patient is not going to make it. That straight, ominous, green line. I had seen it on Charlie's monitor and I knew. The doorway I had been pushed through didn't just mean I was leaving Charlie's hospital room. I was being shoved through a new threshold: The Widow Door.

Collapsing on a bench in a glass walkway that connected one part of the hospital to another, I was only twenty-five yards from Charlie's room but it felt like a chasm separated us. Heaving, I thought, *Now?* *After all this?* After how far we had come to save him, Charlie was going to die *now* on a random Thursday eating dinner in a *hospital?* After all our worries about not being more than an hour away from a major medical center, he was going to die eating grilled chicken *in the Mayo Clinic?*

I don't know how long I was in the hallway. A nurse brought me a glass of water, and then she hurried back to Charlie's room. It seemed the whole hospital was in Charlie's room.

Save him. I thought. *Please save him.*

Don't you walk to that bright light, Charlie, not now. Don't you dare walk toward any bright lights. You see any bright, white light you turn around, damn it. You come back to us. You fight to stay here.

The door to his hospital room burst open and a sea of blue scrub uniforms rushed past with Charlie's body floating at the center. This time, I couldn't see him or touch him. The wave of blue crashed past me, over me, and swept by without me. It was not a cerulean sea. It was a tar-black, salty sea of despair and I began to drown.

I was still alone and sobbing to myself when a nurse gently sat down with me on the bench and put her arm around my shaking shoulders.

How long had I been there? I don't know.

All I remember is that I could hear her saying, "He's alive."

Charlie was still alive.

They had restarted his heart. She didn't know what happened. She didn't know if he would be okay. *But he was alive.*

I had been miraculously pulled back through The Widow Door and I was once again in The Waiting Room. The woman guided me back to what had been Charlie's actual hospital room. It was empty now except for the recliner I had been sitting in only moments before. My iPhone was still where I had abandoned it and the screen blinked with several missed texts from Lauren.

You ready for dinner?

You feel like Italian or steak?

Should I come over?

Mom?

Stay at the hotel. I texted back. *Let's go a little later.*

I couldn't text what really happened.

Your dad died, Lauren.

He died but he came back to us.

He's still alive. You still have a dad.

I sat alone in the empty room where only minutes before Charlie had been eating dinner. I stared at the blank beige wall. I didn't call the girls. I didn't call our families. I didn't know what I would say. I didn't have any words for what had just happened. I was waiting in the blank beige room, but I didn't know what I was waiting for. To be told Charlie was alive but brain-dead?

Everything vital in the room had been removed, most dramatically, Charlie's body. It was amazing how big a hospital room is without a patient in it. All the space that had been filled with the bed, the IV poles, the monitors, even the tray with Charlie's dinner, swept from the room like evidence removed from the scene of a crime. I was alone to bear witness.

That is how the priest found me. I was contemplating the emptiness of the wiped room. When there is a Code Blue in a hospital, apparently they call a priest. This man clad in black with only his white collar as credentials, entered the room not knowing who I was or what had happened. He was the on-call priest simply doing his duty by answering the hospital page. Rolling a chair from the nurses' station, he entered my empty, beige world and sat across from me expectantly. We looked at each other, two strangers, wondering where to begin. He didn't know what happened, and I didn't know where to start.

But it seemed to me, I was alone with God.

I wasn't easy on that priest or God. Thinking about it now, I should have been grateful. I should have fallen to my knees in gratitude for the most precious life, once more miraculously saved. But at the time, that was not how I felt. I was still holding on to all I wanted to be true. I wanted cures. I wanted certainty. I wanted off this terrifying medical roller coaster. And so, I railed and ranted at that priest. Because I could not rail and rant at God, I did it to that priest.

Every frustration, every anger at Charlie's blindsiding crash with rare disease, I let out on that poor priest. Every night of the past four years worrying if I was going to be a widow, I spewed onto him. He had no idea what I was talking about. He had no idea what I meant when I said the word "SCAD." He didn't understand "sarcoidosis." He didn't know about "black swan" cardiac events or sleepless nights vigilantly watching a chest move up and down. All that faith in action that I thought I had found through building homes for the homeless, I lost it. Every bit of wisdom and faith I had thought I had brought home with me from the Camino, it left me.

The priest didn't even try to follow what I was saying. He just let me wail. He let me howl.

He held space with me and allowed me to rage at God.

He was doing exactly as Rachel Held Evans suggested, "*We are called to enter into one another's pain, anoint it as holy, and stick around no matter the outcome.*"

The priest was still with me when a nurse came to get me, "You can see him now."

Jumping up, I began texting Lauren as I hurried down the hall toward the ICU.

Come over to the hospital.

We will have dinner later.

Dad's OK now but he had a problem.

I didn't even say goodbye to the priest. Whether I understood it then or not, he was performing the holiest of tasks—letting me know I was not alone.

Charlie was sitting up in his ICU bed once more swallowed by tubes, but now, the green line on his heart monitor was waving steadily over his right shoulder. It had been only ninety minutes, but Charlie seemed to have aged one hundred years. He looked so fragile that I wanted to wrap my arms around him, but I was afraid to touch Charlie in case the alarms might once again blare.

"What happened?" he murmured through colorless lips.

"I don't know," I said, and saying the words made me start crying all over again.

I still didn't know what happened. Charlie was eating dinner in bed. Then, he was gone. Some kind of medical miracle had brought him back. Again. It seemed Charlie had tried to die at least twice now. Three times if we counted that his stents had failed. But my rare Goose was still here. As upset as I had been with that priest and as mad as I was with God, the fact was, Charlie was still amazingly alive. I felt like the lone witness to that wonder.

In the hours after, we would learn that what happened to Charlie was described as yet another rare event. Another, "one in a million," "never happens" in the medical world, happened to Charlie.

Maybe even more uncommon than SCAD, the event that made Charlie's heart stop, is referred to as an "R-on-T phenomenon." The first doctor who told us about it stood at the end of Charlie's bed shaking his head.

"I've never seen one," he told us. "You hear about it in med school. They told us to hope it never happens because most likely it will mean your patient is dead."

He explained that in order to get the heart back into rhythm, cardiac patients sometimes need to receive a small therapeutic shock. That is what the resident and the nurse had been doing in Charlie's room. Through the electrodes in Charlie's chest, they were delivering this electric bump to help steady his heartbeat. The shock they were sending can hit anywhere in the patient's heart rhythm, but the timing is crucial.

The pulse sent should never arrive at the exact split second that the patient's heart rhythm has the "T wave," which is the tall spike seen on an EKG. If the shock happens at that exact moment, the patient will most certainly die. The chances of that shock hitting in that millisecond as the T-wave ascends are so remote, so rare, that medical students learn about it, but it hardly ever happens. Except to Charlie.

All of the alarms, all of the sirens, and all the personnel who swarmed to save him, all of that had miraculously worked. The crash cart they brought in had jump-started Charlie's heart and brought him back to life. Doctors explained how there could have been multiple complications from Charlie's latest extraordinary emergency yet there seemed to be few aftershocks. Charlie's wounded chest—still incredibly fragile from open-heart surgery—could have been damaged from the dozens of cardiac compressions emergency staff made as they restarted his heart. Yet no ribs had been broken.

Also remarkable, Charlie's lungs—already comprised with sarcoidosis—had not been punctured in the crush to save his life. Any of the dozens of fresh internal stitches or his newly placed cardiac artery could have torn, yet they had all remained strong. Even the brain damage that might have resulted from that menacing flat line, appeared to have been avoided. Tests indicated that Charlie's cerebral function was completely normal. And most miraculous of all, Charlie's heart that had been in mortal danger three times in four years, was beating once again.

"I can't explain why this happened to you, Charlie," our pulmonologist friend. Dr. Craig Daniels said shaking his head. "But I do know, you are really lucky."

Charlie was beyond lucky. We were beyond lucky that day. The past four years we were beyond lucky. So many doctors had helped save Charlie's life over and over. People we knew the names of, like Dr. Omar Ali, Dr. Jane Harrell, Dr. Sharonne Hayes, and Dr. Craig Daniel. And so many others I didn't know, like the nurse who had wheeled in that crash cart or the doctor who pumped Charlie's chest so diligently and carefully that he brought him back to life without damage.

I cannot believe, then or now, that there was a direct intervention from God that made all this so. That would be to believe God had somehow chosen to reach down and save my husband's life over someone else's in the Mayo Clinic that day. Somewhere in those long hallways at the same time Charlie was breathing a new breath, someone else was taking their last. As I was howling my first wails as a momentary widow, some wife or husband had not received the same reprieve. I had suffered for only an hour what I would experience the day Charlie actually died. My preview showed me that day will be excruciating, unending, unrelenting. But that day would not be that day.

While I didn't believe there was a direct hand of God saving Charlie, I did believe in the many human hands who had worked together that day and so many days of the last four years. Hundreds of unknown healthcare heroes performing quiet miracles. I also believed in Charlie's own will, struggling mightily to remain here with us. And I remembered and believed in the prayers both that day and so many times in the previous four years asking for help and hoping that the answer would mean more time for us together. All of that connecting to the divine grace running through this world, healing us all.

For reasons I will never be able to fully fathom, we were given more time while so many like our friend, Steve, or beloved author, Rachel Held Evans, were not. There was also no more time granted to renown Irish poet, theologian, and philosopher, John O'Donohue, who inspired millions with his writing which infused ancient Celtic spirituality to soothe our modern anxiety. Although he had no idea his life on this earth would last only fifty-two years, O'Donohue had already published eight books full of the wisdom and wonder of the world. In *To Bless the Space Between Us: A Collection of Invocations and Blessings*, O'Donohue wrote:

> *We seldom notice how each day is a holy place*
> *Where the eucharist of the ordinary happens,*
> *Transforming our broken fragments*
> *Into an eternal continuity that keeps us.*

While Charlie and I might not have recognized it as it was happening, each day of the past four years had been holy and each moment a gift. The difficulty in this world is to recognize that and live it all at once in the same moment, whether it is our most sorrowful hour or our most joyful one.

12

BELIEVING

UNDER A CANOPY OF
BLESSINGS AND GRACE

Full of the wonder of survival, it is easy to believe in God. Miraculous recoveries match the promise of the church and the resurrection story. It is the suffering that is harder to reconcile with a God who might allow it.

In an interview with Kate C. Bowler on the podcast, *Everything Happens,* author Sarah Bessey admitted, "If you have no theology for suffering, no theology for grief, no theology for wilderness, then you do feel like God's absent because the God that you had constructed or the God that was constructed for you has literally disappeared like steam on a mirror."

That is what I struggled with in the months after Charlie's Code Blue. While Charlie had miraculously lived, we were still chained to two rare diseases with no hope for recovery and no possibility of remission. Unlike recovering cancer patients, we didn't have a specified progress goal, like hoping for a good scan. Like most rare diseases, living with SCAD meant there was no cure. This felt both relentless and hopeless.

It was difficult to imagine only the year before, we thought Charlie might somehow "outgrow" SCAD. It also seemed difficult to remember our "Three for Thirty" Kairos joy. My deeply logical brain insisted it was wishful thinking to pray for a miracle cure for Charlie's two incurable diseases. But to live with no hope, just waiting for Charlie to die, was simply too bleak an existence. I needed to find that final bridge between the reality of science and the hope of faith. Like the Japanese masters of Kintsugi, I needed some golden glue to repair our shattered world and believe in the stronger, more beautiful version of our lives.

In his memoir, *I've Seen the End of You*, neurosurgeon Dr. Lee Warren wrestles with his faith as he operates again and again on patients with the always fatal glioblastoma diagnosis. How could he offer prayers for his patients who he knows will not recover?

Dr. Warren writes:

The more I work around people who are sick and dying, injured beyond repair, or struggling with the hard things life brings, the more I realized something critical: one of the secrets to surviving the difficulties of life is to be honest with yourself about their effect on you.

While Charlie was the patient with two rare diseases, I was the caregiver wrestling daily with little hope. I needed to be honest about how much I was struggling, and I needed someone who might be able to explain God to me.

Charlie's recovery from the open-heart procedure was not progressing as promised. While doctors had indicated a four-to-six-month timeline, we were way past that and 2017 was mired in frustration and depression. My once-smiling, athletic, tanned, fearless husband had become a brooding, thin, pale, fear-filled version of himself. I felt as depleted as the night after his open-heart surgery, and I still felt desperately alone.

As much as I had found some peace in my evolving faith, I was shaken. Watching Charlie struggle over and over just felt overwhelmingly grim. My bones were weighted with daily fears of his impending death and there was nothing I could say to convince myself to lift that terror. My momentary grieving after Charlie had flatlined was becoming my day-to-day living—as if I was already resigned to my eventual fate as a widow whether Charlie was alive or not. Even walking in my magical spiritual park was not working. More often than not, I just cried when I took Dexter to walk our circles, which used to be soothingly sacred.

I had lost all feeling of *Kairos* living and I was squarely back on the tick, tick, tick of *Chronos* time just waiting for Charlie to die. Maybe the truth was, I didn't believe God could help me anymore. The idea of God felt very faraway in the unreachable heavens when I needed a God truly present with me every day dawning on this earth. I wasn't hoping for a miraculous cure, but after four years of uncertainty, I needed to be certain of something. What kind of God kept us, and so many other families with rare diseases, in medical misery and mystery?

Despondent, I made an appointment at our church with Reverend Lisa Saunders. Since she was the powerful architect behind the band of love around Steve's home, I thought she might be able to offer some spiritual direction.

"How are you?" Lisa asked when I entered her office. "How is Charlie?"

We sat facing each other and our knees almost touched. I shrugged not sure where to begin. Through all his struggles, I had never asked for Charlie to be on the church prayer list or receive any clergy visits. Charlie said that made him feel like some kind of declining invalid and as far as he was concerned, his health was a very private subject. In order for her to understand my hopelessness, there was so much that I needed to tell Lisa. Beginning with four years ago, I described our crash with SCAD, then sarcoidosis, then the open-heart surgery, and finally our latest trauma, his R-on-T phenomenon. *Phenomenon.* It struck me as I said it. Not "R-on-T syndrome" but *phenomenon.*

"I can't take it anymore when doctors say 'rare' or 'one in a million',"
I told her. "If it is 'one in a million' that definitely means Charlie has it
or will get it."

As I collapsed in tears and frustration, Lisa allowed me to rant. Just
as the priest at Mayo had held space with me to allow me to howl. But
Lisa wasn't a stranger, she knew my history. She knew all about my decision to quit my job ten years ago to pursue a call to help house the
homeless.

"Maybe I thought that by 'doing good' with my life, you know, working with the homeless, that I would somehow get a hall pass," I told her.
"Maybe that is why I am so scared and so angry. I already lost my dad,
and now I could lose Charlie, too? I did everything I thought I was supposed to do."

Lisa remained quiet but watched me intently as if she was waiting for
me to solve my own riddle.

"I quit my job for a higher purpose—I found faith in that work," I
protested.

"And how does that make you feel now? she asked. "About what you
are going through with Charlie?"

It took a moment, but the picture was starting to fill in for me like
a page in a coloring book where I was beginning to shade between the
lines, giving the image more depth.

"I guess I believed that might mean bad things wouldn't happen to
me," I admitted. "To us and to our family. That maybe my good works
and trying to live a good life would somehow protect us."

Lisa nodded in understanding.

This idea that good conduct could ward off bad outcomes was an
old lie in my life—one I had developed as a little girl. If I was good, Mom
would not go away to the hospital anymore. I tricked myself into believing *that* was in my control. My behavior, my "goodness," was directly
linked to actions in the world as if there was a scorecard somewhere that

was my evidence of my individual merit. Like the original pilgrims on the Camino believing they could present their passport from walking the Way to St. Peter at the Pearly Gates. Hadn't I spent a lifetime walking on the good side of the road? Hadn't Charlie?

The last four years I had felt as if we were receiving the opposite of reward. I felt as if we were somehow sentenced to a life of unending medical misery and our daily punishment was imminent death. Didn't life operate like a bank—if I made deposits of "good" did it not prevent withdrawals of "bad" without my consent?

"Everything happening to Charlie," I told Reverend Lisa Saunders, "makes me feel like we are cursed."

There, I had said it. That is what I could not explain to that priest at the Mayo Clinic. The reason I was so angry with God was because I felt cursed. Despite all the faith I had found in my purposeful life of housing people and developing new spiritual practices, deep down I really only believed in a theoretical God—not a practical everyday God. I didn't believe there was a God walking this Way with me.

While I wasn't expecting a cure, I at least wanted our scorecard to start balancing differently. I wanted all those perceived good deeds I thought had accumulated to count for something. I wanted some assurances that Charlie was not going to die tomorrow from a dissected artery or a spot on his lung. I wanted a life with no broken bodies and no broken minds. A life where we were certain Charlie would one day meet his grandchildren. A life where we would surely grow old together, two, wrinkly, gray-haired, soul mates holding hands in a cabin in Wyoming. I wanted my scorecard to be the guarantee of that life—a life full of certainties and happy endings.

Lisa waited patiently as I wrestled with all that had been said and all that remained unsaid. Soft, brown bangs rested above her glasses and she gazed kindly back at me. I didn't really believe there was anything she could say that could make me feel better, but I needed someone to hear me. I didn't really believe she could release a single pound of the pressure crushing my soul, yet when Reverend Lisa Saunders spoke, she did just that.

"I believe you are living under a canopy of blessings and grace," she almost whispered to me.

"What?" I asked, trying to understand how all that I had just spewed added up to anything but anger and bitterness.

"When I think of all that has happened, each time Charlie should have died, instead he lived," she reminded. "I believe you are living under a canopy of blessings and grace."

I turned those words over in my mind. *Canopy of blessings and grace.*

As if a vice grip had been choking my heart, Lisa's words dissolved my frustration and allowed gratitude to begin seeping back in. Her image of resting in the 'shade of grace' reminded me of the trees in the park that brought me peace. And the sixty-foot oaks in our own backyard that for two decades had shaded Charlie as he moved beneath them with his divine dog parade of one.

I thought about the ambulance driver who had driven the wrong way down the bridge in Massachusetts to get Charlie to the hospital in time. I thought about Dr. Omar Ali who happened to be at that cardiac lab and was uniquely skilled to stent Charlie's shredded, failing artery. I thought about the amazing trinity of Dr. Jane, Dr. Sharonne Hayes, and Dr. Craig Daniels, who constantly conferred to keep Charlie as well as he could be. I thought about the sarcoidosis that remained only in Charlie's lungs and had not spread to his eyes, kidneys, or heart. I thought about the pain in Charlie's arms, which remains a gracious warning signal alerting us to danger before his stents catastrophically fail. And I thought about that R-on-T phenomenon which had not, beyond all logic, taken Charlie's life or left residual damage.

Every single instance of peril had led to a next chance. Another chance at this life. Another chance of one more day together in a marriage of more than thirty-four years. Another chance to spend one more day with our four daughters in this, our sacred circle of six.

Lisa was so right. We were far from cursed. We were remarkably, beyond all reasonable odds, still living in our own gorgeous shade of grace.

Richard Rohr writes, "We do not think ourselves into new ways of living, we live ourselves into new ways of thinking."

I had been thinking of it all wrong and, thus, I had been living it all wrong. I could choose to wake up and wallow in worry of becoming a widow, or I could choose to live openly in receipt of each day remaining in this life with Charlie. I had been given a reprieve. I had been given more time. And I had been wasting every minute of it. In my mind, Rohr sums it all up with this:

But they keep doing their own kind of survival dance,
because no one has told them about their sacred dance.

With rare diseases, with cancer, with cardiac trauma, there is so much surviving that must happen. The appointments, the treatments, the surgeries, and the endless prodding of needles. Whether we are the patient in pain or the caregiver absorbing the hurt of those we love, in the slog of survival we forget why we are trying to live in the first place. We forget why we are trying to steal one more blissful breath under our amazing canopy of blessings and grace. We are the only witnesses to our own wonder.

And so it becomes a choice. We have to choose to pay attention. We have to choose what matters. We have to choose how to spend our days. If we are going to do the work of repairing our lives, one of the most important ingredients in creating the golden glue is choosing to recognize the blessings and grace surrounding us all.

RETURNING

There is nothing so whole as a broken heart.

KOTZER REBBE

13

CHOOSING

FINDING WHAT MATTERS
IN THIS WORLD

In the final process of a labyrinth walk, there is always the Returning. Whatever journey we have been on, whatever old beliefs we have Released and whatever wisdom we have Received, we must each then Return and decide: how will we live?

This Returning always involves choosing. Particularly when we realize our mortality comes with a timeline, so choices must be made. Charlie and I needed to decide how we wanted to spend our time and who we wanted to spend our precious hours with.

Author David Brooks describes this idea in his book, *Second Mountain: The Quest for a Moral Life*. A popular writer and columnist for *The New York Times*, Brooks gained new perspective not through a crisis of health but a crisis of faith. In an interview with *The Atlantic* Brooks wrote:

> *I wanted to make faith, and the journey towards faith, seem very ordinary. There's nothing super miraculous and there are no dramatic moments. There's just a gradual suffusion, a gradual understanding.*

In *Second Mountain*, Brooks tells the stories of people who have shifted their perspectives from what was important during the first part of their lives ("first mountain") to the second half ("second mountain"). Through his research Brooks discovered, "The goals of the first mountain are the normal goals our culture endorses—to be a success, to be well thought of, to get invited into the right social circles, and to experience happiness. Then something happens. They sense there must be a deeper journey they can take."

Through our journey with rare disease, Charlie and I had each been changed. But we were going to need to risk being disturbed to make a deeper journey.

If his two rare diseases meant we did not have decades left together, I wanted to make different choices. But Charlie and I were continuing to disagree about how best to spend the time he had.

Charlie had been doubling down at work, trying to return to the guy he had been, the one who came into the office first and left last. But it wasn't going as he planned. Nine months after his open-heart surgery, Charlie still had little stamina and, by the weekend, the only thing he wanted to plan was a nap. His career in a complex financial world used to energize him, but now it drained him. He took time out to walk or golf, but he was tired all the time. Charlie was trying to return to who he used to be—the guy who worked hard, played hard, and worked harder. But that was not who he was anymore. His body wouldn't let him be that guy.

Our differences came to a head the weekend we were supposed to go to a wedding in Asheville. The son of one my best friends was getting married and there was no way I was going to miss that happy event. Charlie's chest had been hurting all week and he had just returned from another visit with Dr. Jane to receive some IV fluids—a protocol that had become a biweekly procedure. Since his surgery, Charlie was constantly dehydrated so he drank daily bottles of saltwater and received intravenous fluids twice a month. During his visit, Dr. Jane had been so concerned about Charlie that she advised him to skip the wedding in order to rest.

Because of his exhaustion, Charlie and I had been having a lot of talks about life. About what was important. About what was next for us. Charlie's heart was stable but his body was weak. His scans for sarcoidosis had shown no further growth, but I was worried. If there was only going to be a finite time together, I was ready for next chapters and to work in earnest on the human "being" part of life instead of human "doing."

I dreamed of traveling with Charlie and filling our memory bank together in case it was all going to come to an end too soon. My desire for Charlie to retire was not only about time together but also about Charlie's stamina. Once he relinquished the stress of his career, I believed Charlie's health would improve. All the stress and constant pressure of his job wasn't working for him. In my mind, Charlie needed to find out why he was still here. I kept hearing what Dr. Jane had told him, "Charlie, you should be dead three times over. You need to find out why God still wants you here."

Charlie was never going to find the answer to that question if he kept trying to be who he used to be. After four years of constant worry and medical trauma, I wanted Charlie to retire and I meant right now.

"I am not a quitter," Charlie protested. "That feels like quitting and giving up."

"It's not quitting, it's choosing," I said. "Choosing a different way of living."

"My dad always said that the guys who retired early ended up dying first because they had nothing to live for," he said. "You can only golf and fish so much."

"You will find something else," I argued. "You can't find who you are meant to be if you are only willing to be who you were."

While his father, Poppop, had found a way to ponder life's questions through deep theological study, Charlie began to find some answers on a river. Before SCAD, Charlie had no interest in fly-fishing because it seemed so sedentary. Why participate in a sport with no sweat. Beginning at a river only a short drive from Charlotte, Charlie was initially frustrated trying to master the proper techniques. With his inherent athletic abilities, however, Charlie's rod soon began to move as fluidly as his lacrosse stick once had. All it took was that first, big, brown trout on his line and Charlie was hooked.

Fly-fishing became Charlie's form of meditation. Casting a line out on the water with Dexter at his side, Charlie found peace in simply being. Like my labyrinth experience had done for me that day, Charlie finally discovered on a river a place where his mind was quiet, his body felt safe, and his soul seemed full. I couldn't believe that a sport he never wanted to try was becoming the sport that was saving him. After a weekend morning spent fishing, Charlie would come back radiating a joy for life that I had not seen since his heli-skiing days. While there is a small adrenalin rush in hooking a beautiful rainbow trout, it was the connection to pure, simple living that was most life-affirming for Charlie.

My biggest fear was that Charlie was going to die at his desk, literally at his desk. That had recently happened to a Charlotte businessman. He was seventy-eight years old, still working, and passed away at his office. It was wholly unexpected and some might say he died doing what he loved. But Charlie sure loved being outside in the mountains fishing with Dexter. If Charlie was going to die young, I would much rather imagine him taking his last breath in a pine-scented forest next to a stream rather than in a downtown office building.

This had been a four-year battle between us and no one was winning. Me saying, enough was enough and Charlie saying he wasn't ready. Me saying work was part of the problem and Charlie saying it was the only way he knew to get up in the morning.

That wedding weekend, I was frustrated that Charlie wouldn't be attending with me and angry that his job was getting every ounce of his energy. There was no fixing it so I resigned myself to attending alone. As I packed, I continued the argument in my head, searching for any argument that might win our long debate. After years of being the protector and the breadwinner, Charlie's overriding fear was that he had to keep working to leave me well-supported if he died soon. No matter how I presented the evidence of our thirty-year savings and my own capacity to earn an income, Charlie argued it was not yet enough. He was convinced he still needed to provide, despite my argument that it was actually costing us our most precious resource—his health.

My best argument was that the stress of his job was actually costing Charlie his health. The case for this was outlined in a book I read called, *Why Zebras Don't Get Ulcers* written by Robert M. Sapolsky, professor of biological sciences, neurology, and neurological sciences at Stanford University. Although the title sounds somewhat flippant, Dr. Sapolsky conducts serious research on stress and neuron degeneration, which in 1987 earned him a MacArthur Fellowship genius grant.

In his book and his many TED talks, Dr. Sapolsky explains how our bodies were designed with a highly tuned "fight or flight" response to save us from impending peril. Like zebras on the plains of Africa, we are wired to sense potential crisis and flee from an impending threat—like say lions. But this same system responds to psychological stress the same as it does physical stress. When under psychological stress, like Charlie's high-pressure financial job, our bodies don't know when to stop warning of an impending danger. We remain on high alert not just for a brief immediate danger (lion!) but for years.

Over time, this causes lasting physical damage, putting us at risk for numerous stress-related diseases and disorders. I couldn't be sure if that was why Charlie had two rare diseases—no one could—but I knew the constant pressure of his profession was not helping. Dr. Sapolsky's book had been suggested to us by a doctor but Charlie had yet to read it.

Loading my suitcase in the car, I came back to kiss Charlie goodbye before I left for Asheville. Hugging him tight around the waist I looked up and told him, "I need you to do something for me while I am gone. I need you to read that Zebra book."

That weekend at the wedding, it was like a dress rehearsal for my deepest fear. It began when I walked into my hotel room and put down my bags, alone. The king-sized bed we had reserved felt impossibly big and the closet held only my dress, not Charlie's suit, making it look lonely on the single hanger. Escaping our room, I tried to reframe the weekend as a retreat. The evening's welcome party would not begin until 9:00 p.m., which meant I had four hours to kill. Settling in at an outdoor café table, I ordered a cheese plate and a glass of wine before opening the novel I brought. But I could not help watching all the couples sharing a Friday night date. My lone glass of wine and the empty chair beside me just magnified Charlie's absence.

Driving to the party that I had no desire to attend solo, I thought about my friends who were divorced, or worse, widowed in their fifties. This is what it was like going to the party without a date, I thought. It had been over thirty years since I had been without a date. I didn't know how to do it anymore. I didn't want to know how to do it.

The party was full of our Charlotte friends, but as I walked in, I felt completely alone. Charlie was not turning to me asking what I wanted to drink. There was no comfort in walking up to a group knowing he was not at my side. Throughout the night I moved from friend to friend, playing the part of the party guest, yet I kept instinctively looking for him, *my Goose.*

Charlie was easy to spot at party because he was always one of the tallest men. I had grown accustomed to searching the crowd to find his handsome profile laughing with the other guests like a lighthouse, no matter how far away, reassuring of home. Throughout a typical evening, I could count on him to come up beside me at different times in the night and lightly touch my back before introducing himself or joining the conversation. I could always coax him onto the dance floor, setting our drinks on a high-top before entering the moving mass of bodies. After three decades, we knew each other's steps. I knew he would twirl me just until the moment I might be slightly dizzy and catch me before I actually fell. That night, I sorely missed my dance partner.

The next day during the ceremony, I sat with my friend during the service, because she, too, was without a date. I teared up watching the bride and groom staring into each other's eyes with the new promise of their life together. It was when they began their vows that I actually started weeping upon hearing the words "*in sickness and in health.*" And a few moments later, there was no hand to grasp as the young couple vowed "*till death do us part.*"

It was a preview of the life I was not willing to live if I had a choice, and I believed we still had a choice. Charlie could choose to walk away. To put his health first. To stop wearing himself out over budgets and bottom lines. To choose making it to next year over making it to the next meeting.

I drove home resolved. I was going to tell Charlie it was time. He had to retire whether he was ready or not because *I was ready.* I needed Charlie to choose our family over some arbitrary finish line. I could not see any other way forward and I was not willing to sign onto one more day watching him die a slow death All two hours and twenty minutes of the drive home, I practiced the words I would say to convince Charlie he had to retire.

When I walked in the door, however, I did not have to explain anything. I had not said a word when Charlie greeted me at the door and pointed to the Zebra book on the counter behind him. Wrapping me in a hug, he bent down to whisper, "I get it," he said, "I am going to do it. I am going to retire."

At the same time, in the same weekend, yet two hundred miles apart, Charlie and I came to the same decision. To stop practicing old steps. To stop doing the survival dance. To stop trying to be who we were instead of who we had become.

The last five years had felt like we had been wandering in the cardiac desert of imminent death. But maybe these years had really been about discovering how to live. About transforming both of us into two people who were not so obsessed with doing but with being. Not so focused on achieving but breathing.

What do two constantly moving, Type A, control freaks need to shake them from their ways but a disease like SCAD that is uncontrollable and unsolvable? A disease that no amount of Googling or persistence could ever possibly solve.

What could make you feel more alive each moment of your life than a disease that could take your life just as fast? Unless the fear of that happening suffocates and steals the very life you've been given. Unless you refuse to let go of what you cannot solve and keep repeating old patterns and old ways of living believing that the tighter you hold on the more you can control.

Maybe the greatest gift any of us can receive in this world is the opportunity to truly understand what a treasure this very day is. To be breathing and living with people we love, choosing each other over and over in this precious life we are given. Miraculously here for this moment until death do us part.

Thomas Merton, an American monk, writer, and theologian wrote:

People may spend their whole lives climbing the ladder of success only to find, once they reach the top, that the ladder is leaning against the wrong wall.

After over thirty years of marriage and four years of SCAD, Charlie and I were finally going to begin looking together for new and better walls. But in that search, we were going to have to risk changing.

Irish poet and priest, John O'Donohue, wrote *A Book of Blessings* with poems and prayers for life's struggles as well as celebrations. His poem, *A Morning Offering*, ends with these two stanzas:

May my mind come alive today
To the invisible geography
That invites me to new frontiers
To break the dead shell of yesterdays,
To risk being disturbed and changed.

May I have the courage today
To live the life that I would love,
To postpone my dream no longer
But do at last what I came here for
And waste my heart on fear no more.

This was our time. This was our moment. We needed to waste our hearts on fear no more.

14

LOVING

LESSONS FROM
A WIDOW

Making new choices looks different for everyone. A diagnosis that causes us to quit our jobs and finally attend to forgotten dreams. A divorce that forces a move to another city. Or maybe losing someone we love simply makes us hold tighter to those around us.

Writer and theologian, Enuma Okoro, discusses her spiritual journey and new life choices in *Reluctant Pilgrim*. In that memoir she writes:

> I know life doesn't always work out easily and that our prayers are not always answered in recognizable ways. I know that making collages does not put an end to cancer or infertility or even to relationship and vocational concerns. I know all these things. Solidly. But I also know that healing takes many forms. Sometimes the parts of our hearts, minds and spirits and bodies that receive healing can look nothing like the healing for which we have prayed. And therein lies the risk, not so much that our prayers fall on deaf divine ears but that we might miss the measure of healing we end up being given.

While Charlie had not been cured, his retirement felt like a piece of the healing I desperately needed. It wasn't until I began writing about our experience that I could fully see how much more there was to the story. I had, as Okoro wrote, "missed the measure of healing we had been given." I still had work to do to reframe the last few years and understand what this life storm had been all about.

The stranger threw her arms around me in an honest embrace and declared "I feel like you are my best friend!" I pulled back from this disarming bear hug to study the woman's face searching for a clue. She went on to tell me, "I feel like I know everything about you!"

We were in the fellowship hall of a local church and this experience, while odd, was also beginning to be a familiar occurrence. It was the beginning of 2018 and my first book, *The Hundred Story Home*, had been released. All my writing, seeking, and processing had finally added up to a published memoir about finding my own way home through housing the homeless.

At first my memoir was only read by my friends, but it had been making its way through book clubs, Sunday School classes, and church mission presentations like this one. While I had written very openly about my faith journey and my childhood experiences with my mother's mental health struggles, that book timeline ended in 2012—the year before Charlie's heart attack. This woman who hugged me so sincerely believed she knew everything about me. But really, she had no idea. She had no clue how we had been shattered and how hard I was trying to repair the pieces since the end of what she had read about my life.

I had not realized how the process of writing that memoir while simultaneously navigating Charlie's very difficult health challenges had been saving my own life. As I spoke to groups, I felt mildly dishonest discussing my 2008 faith story when I knew our current battle with SCAD was the real-time story. My friend, Edwina, had encouraged me to write about Charlie. "This is going to help so many other people," she said with certainty. But I couldn't imagine writing about it when I felt we were still drowning in it. We had barely survived each of his cardiac emergencies, and I knew there was still a possibility he could have another. I couldn't write a book to "help so many" when frankly, I was the one who needed help.

While Charlie was designing his retirement, I was still looking for my next chapter. Since I loved writing, I had made a promise to myself: attend at least one writing seminar a year. Maybe that way I would find my way to another subject to write my next book. After researching options online, I was intrigued by this workshop title: *Listening to Your Story*. Hooked by this title and the location (Santa Fe, New Mexico), I signed up immediately.

As I settled into my boutique adobe hotel, I had the same buzz of anticipation I had experienced before embarking on the Camino. It seemed all of Santa Fe resonated with spirituality. Beneath the mountains gathered all types of people exploring both outdoor adventures and inner journeys. When I Googled "History of Santa Fe Spirituality," dozens of entries popped up. I had not realized that the divine significance of this New Mexican community dated back centuries. Even more surprising in my online exploration, I discovered that a mere thirty minutes from Santa Fe was a world-class pilgrimage site: El Santuario de Chimayo.

The website for this famous site stated that an estimated 300,000 people a year trek to this small chapel that was thought to be the site of a miracle centuries before. Now, the sanctuary is a sacred destination for thousands of pilgrims seeking a surprising treasure inside the small chapel: dirt. I reread the meaning of that sentence twice.

People from all over the world come for the dirt.

Holy Healing Dirt meant for spiritual and physical transformation.

I had never heard of Chimayo or Holy Healing Dirt. Since I had traveled thousands of miles to Spain last year for a pilgrimage, I thought I should at least attempt to make the thirty-minute drive to see this famous chapel. When I researched the visiting hours, however, it proved to be impossible. My writing workshop was a full day—9:00 a.m. to 5:00 p.m. The Chimayo chapel was a thirty-minute drive and closed at 6:00 p.m. The timing simply did not work. Next time I was in Santa Fe, I vowed to check out this fantastical dirt.

On the first morning of our workshop, I nervously entered the classroom, selecting a seat which ended up being right next to our instructor, Margaret Wrinkle, author of the acclaimed novel, *Wash*. With shoulder-length, gray-streaked hair, Margaret was dressed simply and I doubted whether she ever cared much about fashion. Her writing indicated she was much more interested in what was on the inside rather than the outside of a person. While she possessed a fairly serious resting face, when she smiled, Margaret instantly transformed from wise woman to impish girl.

Over our first two days, Margaret mixed writing exercises with meditation, a process which produced surprising results for each of us novice writers. As we read our in-class writing, we shared aloud in wonder. Stories appeared on our pages that we had no idea were buried inside. Margaret nodded knowingly that this process of spiritual writing had a way of revealing inner truths. We were eight strangers who quickly became intimate friends by sharing our words.

When I signed up for this class months before, I knew I had to submit fifteen pages of unpublished work. Other than the memoir I had just published, the only piece of writing I had finished was more of an extremely personal journal entry. Four months before in February 2018, I had written this very unexpected piece. It happened while Charlie and I were on a fishing weekend that had a significant date: the five-year anniversary of his first SCAD.

While Charlie was outside on a freezing river, I had chosen to stay inside. Nestled into a chair, I began allowing words I had never thought I would write to spill out onto the page. My hands could not stop typing fast enough about that fateful day when our world had changed. I wrote almost 3,000 words in one sitting and my unexpected essay began:

> *If I had to pick a moment, one moment where normal morphed into surreal, I would have to say it began with a turkey sandwich in a quaint New England café seven states away from where my husband, Charlie, and I call home.*

It was like a purging of my soul, telling the truth of what had happened to us. After I was through, I saved the document and closed my computer unsure of what to do with the three chapters I had just written. I had not even gone back to reread my words until I needed to submit something for the Santa Fe workshop. Since I had no other essays written, I sent the pages to the instructor, Margaret, without much thought.

I had not really considered what that would mean. My very intimate thoughts about the most devasting day in my life would be read aloud and critiqued by strangers. I had never even let Charlie read the pages. In fact, I rarely spoke about that day except to my therapist. Sitting in the workshop, hearing each painful word read aloud by Margaret and discussed by eight writers, I began to know. I began to know those fifteen pages were my next subject. I began to know, without a doubt, it was the beginning of the next book I must write. And at the same time I knew, without a doubt, I didn't want to write it.

Writing that book would mean I would not only reveal the abyss we had inhabited the past few years, I would have to relive that time in order to write about it. Most terrifying of all to contemplate was, that book would need an ending. All books must have an ending and that was the real problem of writing this story. I didn't want to write the logical ending.

Charlie was going to die and I was going to be alone.

That was the only way a story about a guy with two rare diseases ends. It was just the hard truth. Maybe not tomorrow. Maybe not next week. But it was coming. I knew in my bones it was coming, but I had not allowed myself to write about it for fear of making it come true. My childhood had taught me not to talk about things like Mom going into a psychiatric hospital. The best way to get through it was to pretend it wasn't happening. Just wake up and move through the day as if it is not happening. Not thinking about hard things will somehow make them easier.

My husband dying and leaving me a young widow? Close my eyes and pretend it was not so and, thus, it wouldn't be. In that Santa Fe workshop as my pages were discussed aloud, there was no pretending it didn't happen or wasn't happening. I could feel the empathy from my fellow writers as they relived our horror from that first cardiac crash. I watched their reactions as they realized, just as Charlie and I had learned five years ago, that arteries can split for no known reason with catastrophic consequences. There was no way to say it wasn't true.

"Wait, you mean this is nonfiction?" one writer asked.

I nodded.

"That was going to be my critique," she said. "I didn't think it was believable. I thought your story was fiction and I was going to tell you I didn't buy it."

Me, too. I wished my story was fiction. I wished I could rewrite the pages and edit them choosing a new disease. One with a long unpronounceable name but after a courageous battle there would be a certain victory.

Charlie could be in remission!

Charlie could be cured!

Charlie could beat the odds!

That uplifting tale could end with us as a pair of eighty-year-olds living in Wyoming fly-fishing together on the shores of a river. That would be an ending to a book I would like to write.

Instead I was listening, as if for the first time, to my own nonfiction story, and it was shocking to hear the truth of our story read aloud. This disease had been haunting us for five years, lurking in the shadows with a heart attack hiding on every corner and a funeral threatening to begin. I was trying to live in the gratitude of the moment but was too scared to go to sleep in case that next day would be the day I woke up a widow.

The brutal honesty of all that hit me in full force as I sat in that workshop *"Learning to Listen to Your Story."* I was certainly learning and listening with eight former strangers who now knew my deepest fears. I felt as if I had been time traveling, seeing the past and the future all in one moment. Charlie's medical saga. What had been. What would be. My life to come: alone.

I could not speak. I could not think. I needed to breathe. The critique of my writing was over and I had barely heard the comments. I needed to get out of that room and away from everyone. Hurrying outside to the courtyard, I collapsed on a smooth, adobe bench which was built in a circle around the trunk of a tall tree.

Canopy of blessings and grace.

Resting in the shade, I looked up at the sky and allowed myself to cry. To weep for the life I wanted but, realistically, I was not going to receive. The one where Charlie and I get to write the ending we choose for our story: forever together celebrating a golden wedding anniversary.

What had always frightened me the most about Charlie dying was where would I go? How could I live in this world now only one half of a whole? Every place I knew reminded me of him. I couldn't live in Charlotte, missing Charlie every moment and feeling a part of me had died as well. I was going to need to find a new, safe place. One where I had a chance to feel if not whole, then at least three-quarters.

Pressed against the tree trunk, looking up at the endless New Mexico sky reminded me of my cathedral of trees in my park in Charlotte. With this view of wide-open sky, I could begin to breathe and a new peace settled on me. While it wasn't the same El Paso desert of my childhood, it had the same feeling of home. A reassuring thought emerged: Santa Fe could be my escape plan. The place I could come to not feel half of a whole. I could imagine myself wrapped in the solace of the Southwest. Closing my eyes, I tried to hold that image of safe space. I tried to inhale the comfort of a plan.

Suddenly, she was beside me: Maria. She was a fellow writer with the most beautiful Irish accent when she read aloud her pages. All week when Maria had read her work, I wanted to just close my eyes and drift into her narrative reality. Sitting down beside me on the adobe bench, Maria cradled my hand in hers and began to speak to me.

"I wanted to tell you something if I may," she said. Her voice was as soothing as a massage, and I wanted to melt into her every word. I nodded and I didn't try to hide the tear sliding down my cheek. I was beyond caring. These people all knew me. All week, they had listened to inner thoughts some of my best friends didn't know. I had nothing left to hide.

"I know, but I don't know, what you are feeling," Maria said. "My husband had pancreatic cancer."

I looked into Maria's face for the first time. For the past few days, I had really only seen her profile as she read. Chin-length hair streaked with wisps of gray and silver, drop earrings that swayed when she read. I'm not sure I had even seen her face before, but it glowed in the Santa Fe sun. Maria's eyes were bright, kind, and framed by smile lines radiating the most generous gaze.

I focused on her words. *Had* pancreatic cancer. Not *has* pancreatic cancer. I knew where she was going with this. Maria was already a widow.

"Listening to you in there, I can tell how much you love your husband," she said. "You have a special relationship."

I nodded, the reservoir of tears spilling over.

"We did, too," Maria said. "Can I ask you something?"

She paused, waiting for my nod before proceeding with her question.

"Is your husband open to the spiritual?" she asked.

I thought a moment. Was he? Maybe. But I had been the one on the faith journey these past few years. I had been the one reading spiritual books, walking a labyrinth, and making my Camino pilgrimage. I had been Releasing, Receiving, and Returning over and over. Charlie accepted that I had found something bigger than myself to believe in, but he was not pursuing spiritual direction in the same way I had been. Although he was pondering life's questions on a river, Charlie had not signed up for years of theological study like his father, Poppop. So far, Charlie was not asking twelve years' worth of questions.

"Not really," I told Maria. "You know, it's not that he is resistant. He is just not as far along this path as I am . . ." and I let the words drift.

She nodded. "My Sam as well. And it bothered me and I wanted him . . . no, I needed him to find some peace before he died. The peace I had."

Maria paused searching my face to see if any of this was making sense. I squeezed her hands in affirmation and she continued. "We

didn't have a church home so we didn't even have a place to hold his
memorial service. But there was a monastery near our house that Sam
thought might be good. He thought it was peaceful but we didn't know
anyone there. One day I saw one of their Buddhist monks in Trader
Joe's. He was buying bananas. . . ."

"A Buddhist monk in Trader Joe's?" I asked with a small, incredulous
laugh.

"Yes," she said smiling at the memory. Together, our giggles broke
the gravity of the moment. Regaining composure, we held each other's
hearts with our eyes before she continued.

"Yes, a monk buying bananas in Trader Joe's. And I said to him
'Father, I want Sam to know. I want him to speak to you,'" Maria said.
"And it helped. It did. Sam talked with him and then, we talked together
and it made everything so much better. Having something to believe
together—it made it so much better."

Her words. Her voice. Her story. They were a balm and a blessing.
They softened the whiplash of clarity that had arrived in the past hour
from the pain in my pages. At the same time I had been listening to
Maria, an inner voice had been rising inside me. It was insisting I had
somewhere to be. It whispered that I must go. I didn't know why but I
knew exactly where it wanted me to go.

"Maria, I just learned about this place. It is a pilgrimage site near
here and they have Holy Dirt," I told her. "Holy Healing Dirt. I know
this might sound crazy and I know your reading is next but I have to get
there before they close. I have to get some Holy Dirt for Charlie."

Maria did not even act surprised. She simply smiled and leaned forward with sincere encouragement, "Go get your dirt!"

We hugged tightly, each knowing someday I would join a type of
club no one really ever wants to belong to. But embracing under that
cottonwood tree, Maria made me believe I would never truly be alone.

Jan Richardson is an author, artist, and young widow, who wrote *The Cure for Sorrow: A Book of Blessings for Times of Grief* (Wanton Gospeller Press, 2020, www.janrichardson.com). In it she offers blessings to soothe the aching hearts of all who love, and then must let go.

A BLESSING FOR
THE BROKENHEARTED

Let us agree
for now
that we will not say
the breaking
makes us stronger
or that it is better
to have this pain
than to have done
without this love.

Let us promise
We will not
tell ourselves
time will heal
the wound,
when every day
our waking
opens it anew.

Perhaps for now
it can be enough
to simply marvel
at the mystery
of how a heart
so broken

can go on beating,
as if it were made
for precisely this—

as if it knows
the only cure for love
is more of it,

as if it sees
the heart's sole remedy
for breaking
is to love still,

as if it trusts
that its own
persistent pulse
is the rhythm
of a blessing
we cannot
begin to fathom
but will save us
nonetheless.

Dr. Sunita Puri is considered an "Uncertainty Specialist" in her role as medical director of palliative medicine at the Keck Hospital and Norris Cancer Center. Raised first-generation American by immigrant parents, her mother was an anesthesiologist and her father an engineer. Together, they raised Sunita to believe in both faith and medical science. "They showed me very early on that God and science are not binaries, that spirituality and science can sit side-by-side in the service of humanity," Dr. Puri said.

In her memoir, *That Good Night: Life and Medicine in the Eleventh Hour*, Dr. Puri encourages doctors and patients alike to fuse medicine with faith for our most powerful healing. Dr. Puri writes:

> *My mother introduced me to human biology and physiology, but she and my father also taught me that the body, imperfect and impermanent, is the home of the soul. And the soul, the eternal sprit within each body is immortal, indestructible, immune to the cycles of birth and death that our mortal bodies experience. We are not these bodies, my parents would tell my brothers and me. We are the souls within. Part of our journey on earth is to learn that birth and death may be the beginning and the end of the body, but not of us. And a spiritual practice can help us to remember the truth of who we are, and to recognize the unified quest of all beings: seeking to understand themselves and their own innate divinity. Doctors could treat disease, my mother told me, but only God could shape the soul's journey. This is why some patients survived when nobody expected they would and others died when their survival was assumed. Prayer, my mother told me, was more powerful than medicine and a necessary part of any treatment plan.*

Despite the study that showed over 90% of Americans use healing prayer, it had never really been a part of my coping strategy. While I had prayed to God often over the past few years, I wasn't really expecting an answer since science assured me there was no cure for SCAD or sarcoidosis. Until I went to Chimayo to get my Holy Healing Dirt, I didn't understand that asking for a cure and seeking healing are two very different prayers.

15

HEALING

PRAYERS FOR
ACCEPTANCE

So many people in the past few years had given me a lifeline just when I needed it most. Maria sharing her story just when I felt most alone. Tammie, my therapist, introducing me to a library of faith writers when I needed deep answers. Reverend Lisa Saunders reminding me of the canopy of blessings and grace when I felt cursed. It seems there are always people on our paths who we are meant to meet. There are always those willing to help us repair the cracks to create the most beautiful and strongest versions of ourselves.

Dr. Mary C. Neal has written two *New York Times* best-selling books about her personal miracle story when she "died" while kayaking on a river in Chile, yet miraculously she resurrected. Full of medical details of her improbable survival, Dr. Neal also writes convincingly of her spiritual encounter and the lessons she learned. In *7 Lessons from Heaven: How Dying Taught Me to Live a Joy-Filled Life*, Dr. Neal writes about "looking within" for connections that trace to God in our story when people or circumstances seem beyond coincidence.

I've found that God shows up in small (or large) miracles, in hard-to-explain synchronicities, or in improbable encounters with people who

nudged me toward my higher purpose. For me, God's sustaining grace
is often most apparent during my darkest days when I have felt most
abandoned and alone.

If we look back, we see in our stories, maybe even in our worst
moment, when someone provided just what we needed. The right words
of encouragement. The name of a lifesaving specialist. Or maybe simply
doing the holy work of being present in our suffering so we would know
we were not alone. Maria had given me just the words I needed to listen to my whisper to take one more pilgrimage. Whether I understood
the reason or not, Maria believed with me that I needed to go to El
Santuario de Chimayo.

Leaving the writer's workshop, I felt as if outside forces were propelling
me forward. I needed to arrive at Chimayo before they closed at 6:00
p.m., yet I still had one call to make.

"Charlie?" I said through the hundreds of miles. He picked up on
the first ring, and without asking, I knew he was sitting at our kitchen
counter eating grilled chicken and green beans.

"Hey! Good day?" he asked.

"Wild day," I answered. I wasn't sure where to begin. The pages I had
written? The conversation with Maria? The quest for Holy Dirt? I felt my
spiritual bubble bursting as it bumped into reality.

How was I going to explain all that I was feeling and all that had
been happening?

"So, we had to submit pages for this workshop and I sent the pages I
wrote in February on our fishing trip. The pages about you," I said confess-
ing that eight strangers had just read what I had still not shared with him.

Thankfully, Charlie did not interrupt.

"And when we were talking about them, I knew. I knew that this is a book I am meant to write but I have been afraid to write," I told him.

"Why are you afraid to write it?" Charlie asked.

I waited. I realized I was crying. I was choking on the words. "Because I am afraid of how it will end," I whispered. "I don't want to write the ending."

I knew. He knew. We both knew what I meant. That a book about a guy with two one-in-a-million rare diseases ends one way: death. Most likely with a fatal heart attack which leaves behind a widow. That's it. That is the way it has always felt this will end. Neither of us knew when that would happen, but it has always been the logical, rational conclusion.

"But then, I left class, and I went to the courtyard and this woman followed me out. And she told me how she didn't know our story but she knew how we felt, because she had just lived it. Her husband just died of pancreatic cancer," I stopped giving pause to that reality. Giving a moment for Maria and Sam and all they had been through and maybe all that Charlie and I had yet to go through.

"And she asked if you were spiritual like me and I told her not really. . . . "

"I think about things more than you think, Kathy," Charlie said a thousand miles away but right beside me.

I smiled. "I know, but you know what I mean. And she said at the end, she really wanted her husband to have some peace. It was really important to her."

I paused gathering courage for the next part.

"Then, one day, she saw this Buddhist monk in Trader Joe's," I said laughing even as I repeated it.

"A Buddhist monk in Trader Joe's?" Charlie cut in.

"Yes, I know it sounds weird. But she asked if her husband could talk with him and he did. And it made it all so much better, because in the end they were in the same place and she knew he was going to be okay," I took a breath. "I need that for you. I need that for us."

I had spit out so many words that I wasn't sure if Charlie was tracking it all, but I kept going.

"And there's this place up the road. It is a world-class pilgrimage site, you know like the Camino? And here it is, thirty minutes away, not like in Spain or anything. And they have dirt. Holy Dirt. And I know I am supposed to go. I know I am supposed to go to get you some Holy Healing Dirt."

Charlie was silent for a moment. I waited. Did he have any idea what I was talking about? I hoped he could follow because I had never been more certain in my life of what I was supposed to be doing.

"Do you have a bag?" Charlie asked.

"What?" I asked. "Why?"

"For the dirt," he said without irony or hesitation. "You are going to need a bag or something to bring home your dirt."

I had never loved my logical, practical husband more than in that moment.

"They have thousands of tourists a year." I said laughing and loving him so much. "I am sure they are set up for this."

"No," Charlie said, and I could see him shaking his head between bites of beans. "You need to take a bag."

Looking down onto the floor of the rental car, there was a gallon-size Ziploc bag that I always used as an inexpensive travel pouch for my computer cords and charger. "Yes, I have a bag," I told him.

I could feel Charlie smiling through the phone in satisfaction.

"Then go get your Holy Dirt," he said.

Checking my watch, it was now after five o'clock so I had less than an hour to get to the sanctuary before they closed. The road to Chimayo was an easy thirty-minute drive that felt like I had been waiting a lifetime to travel. It was part highway and part New Mexican farmland with adobe homes dotting the sides of the rural road. Passing a series of small ranch houses, a hand-painted four-foot sign with large black letters proclaimed loudly on the side of the road:

God is Not Dead.

Smiling at this randomly placed roadside message, I had to agree. Once I started paying attention, God certainly seemed to be showing up in mysterious ways.

When I crested the last section of the drive heading into the small village of Chimayo, the view was breathtaking. I could see all the way to the horizon, a gently sloping road threading between two symmetrically placed mesas rising into an azure sky.

Arriving at the parking lot, there were only two other cars on the marked pavement designed for hundreds of visitors. It was like an under-attended spiritual theme park. It felt both eerie and extraordinary all at once to have arrived at this popular pilgrimage site only to find it deserted. Signs attached to a chain-link fence reminded in all capital letters:

THIS IS A SACRED PLACE.
PLEASE RESPECT OTHER
VISTORS' DEVOTIONALS.

A walkway beckoned and I followed the sidewalk up an incline bordered by a chain-link fence dividing a multi-acre campus. Tied to this silver fencing were hundreds of rosaries and ribbons which were fluttering in the high mountain desert breeze. When I reached the top of the hill, there was a terra cotta bench in front of a six-foot-wide arched stone altar covered in a kaleidoscope of color created by the hundreds of beaded rosaries left by visitors.

As I walked in silence the final hundred yards of my New Mexican pilgrimage, I realized that in my rush to arrive I hadn't stopped for the practical—a bathroom. I was in one of the stalls when I remembered that I had also forgotten my Ziploc bag in the rental car, but I didn't have time to go back for it. Searching the restroom for a substitute, I saw near the long row of sinks, a crumbled blue-and-white Dixie cup. Seemingly clean and empty, I folded the waxed paper cup into my jean pocket just in case Charlie was right and that I did, in fact, need to bring my own container for my Holy Dirt. I hurried to the chapel hoping it had not already closed for the day.

Stepping into the legendary El Santuario de Chimayo, the ceilings were higher than they appeared from the rounded adobe exterior and not at all like the glorious, soaring rafters of so many cathedrals in Spain. Sliding silently onto one of plain wooden benches, my eyes adjusted to the dim lighting.

Pressing my back against the pew, I paused, closed my eyes, and felt the presence of the thousands who had come reverently before me. I am sure most of those pilgrims had known exactly why they were there and might have planned for years to make their journey. My pilgrimage, however, had started only an hour before, thus I felt both propelled and perplexed as to what exactly I was doing at Chimayo.

While I had come for the Holy Dirt, I wasn't even sure where to find it, or really, what I would do once I did. From the photos on the website, I knew I was looking for a small stone room. Rising from the pew, I made my way to the front of the chapel to a door off to the left of the altar. As I crossed this threshold, there was another low stone doorway to my right. My heart pounded as I realized, I had found it: the stone room with the Holy Dirt.

Ducking under the low archway to enter, I was startled to discover I was alone in this sacred place. I was alone with this famous Holy Dirt. The only light came from one window on the back wall of the small stone space. If I stretched out my arms, I might have been able to touch the walls on either side.

In the middle of the room was a fifteen-inch hole carved into the stone floor revealing the soft, sacred sand. Resting in the seemingly ordinary light-brown dirt was a silver garden spade with a black handle marked by a thumb-sized yellow dot. That was all—just the spade and the dirt. There were no containers and no bags to take it home. I smiled. *Charlie had been right.*

Pulling the crumpled Dixie cup from my jean pocket, I scooped a spadeful into my cup, and then crouched cross-legged on the floor next to the Holy hole. The room was so small it was easy to rest my back against the adobe wall and still be directly beside the center of the earth. Cradling my Holy Cup of Dixie in both hands, I closed my eyes.

Three hundred thousand visitors a year in a place deemed "the most important Catholic pilgrimage site in the United States" yet, somehow, I was here alone. Leaning against the adobe, it felt like a homecoming. With the cup protected beneath my bent knees, I pressed my palms onto the cool ground. My fingertips were pulsing so that it seemed my heartbeat was connecting directly through the stone into the soul of the earth. In the stillness of this altar, the prayers that came to me were words I didn't know I needed to say.

In my heart, I think my intention had been to ask for a cure for Charlie's incurable diseases or for a miraculous intervention for his heart. The prayers I whispered, however, began with Charlie, yet became for me. To heal myself. To begin living again. To alter the life plans and trust the life path. To have faith there was so much more than I could possibly understand.

What filled my heart and soul in that small stone room was the certainty of what Reverend Lisa Saunders had already shown me. I didn't need to come to Chimayo to pray for miraculous healing because the miracles had already happened—several times over in fact. Living so full of fear, Charlie and I had never fully appreciated all that had happened. We had been holding our collective breath for over five years. Waiting for death. Waiting for the worst-case scenario. I had come to plead for more time without understanding that was the wrong request. It was as Enuma Okoro had written: *Sometimes the parts of our hearts, minds and spirits and bodies that receive healing can look nothing like the healing for which we have prayed.*

The words that overflowed inside me beside the Holy Dirt were not about cures. They were about gratitude and love and acceptance. About receiving the blessing of all the extra time we had already been given. About offering thanks for each moment that remained. Charlie was miraculously alive and we shared a love that was as rare as the disease that threatened to steal it.

How many times had I been shown this same lesson? Not only each time Charlie survived, but in the peace of my park, in the *Kairos* of Italy, and along the path of the Camino. These epiphanies that I kept allowing to fade from memory once the *Chronos* tick-tock of life resumed. Each time I walked on the labyrinth path of life, I must remember again to Release and Receive before I Return to begin the process yet again. With each day, I must choose anew whether to spend my life spiraling outwards alone, fearing for the future or winding inwards toward God, present in each moment, profoundly marking what is most true.

As I opened my eyes, the hole in the ground before me seemed to mirror the sinkhole I had so long felt inside me. In that sacred room, my inner sinkhole—just like that hole overflowing with soft sand—felt completely filled with the Holy. I might have arrived a skeptic, but I was leaving a believer. As I carefully protected my Holy Cup of Dixie with my hands, I had full faith in all the potent powers of Chimayo, because it had already healed me. It had given me peace. It had given me certainty. It had given me an ending I was finally willing to write.

If I had learned anything over the past five years, it was that there was a profound difference between finding a cure and being healed. Even when there is a 100% medical certainty of no cure, both the patient and the caregiver need healing. So much theology offers a gospel of good news but more vital is a creed for the incurable. Faith for the fatal. Belief through the bad news.

Instead of everlasting life and modern medicine miracles, we need to change our prayers to include those small, overlooked gifts of grace. We might not receive exactly what we hoped and prayed for, but when we are watchful, we are always receiving grace. Witnessing love at a wedding we never thought might happen. Holding our first grandchild. Reconciling with an estranged family member. None of us has forever but we have this day to wholly embrace.

Kate Bowler, associate professor of the History of Christianity at Duke Divinity School, had to reframe everything she knew when she was diagnosed with Stage IV cancer. She chronicled that crossing in her best-selling memoir *Everything Happens for a Reason (and Other Lies I've Loved)*. In her popular podcast, Kate Bowler interviews people who have experienced all manner of love and loss. To her listeners, Kate wrote:

> *For you who haven't been healed, for you, whose miracle hasn't come, for you, who wince and cringe when no one is looking. For you who find that getting out of bed most mornings is just too hard, for you who have more bad days than good. For you who sit among the shards of unanswered prayer. You are not forgotten. You are not skipped over. You are*

*not alone. Yes, we are united by joy and united by love. But we are also
united by our suffering and by our fragility and by how delicate we all
are. Today, may you experience the relentless love of God. May you be
ruthless in your search for goodness and hope and joy, even as your world
shrinks. May you know that your very flesh and bones is God's home.
And it is good.*

Sometimes it seems as if prayers are unanswered, yet maybe, the
shattering we experience is a breaking open for new possibility. It was
precisely the shattering of life as I knew it that broke open my life for
new possibilities. While our bodies will inevitably break without our
consent, we can attain healing of our minds and restoration of our souls.
We come into this world loving, open, and whole, so despite unwanted
diagnoses and unfair outcomes, we can choose to return to the simple
joy of being alive.

Leonard Cohen was a poet and novelist before he became a singer-
songwriter at age thirty-three, and his career stretched into his eighties.
He was most well-known for the gorgeous ballad "Hallelujah," but it was
the lyrics in "Anthem," of which he was most proud.

"I think it is one of the best songs I have written, maybe the best,"
Cohen told music critic Robert Hilburn in 1995.

Leonard Cohen took over a decade to complete "Anthem" for two
reasons. First, part of the song was mistakenly erased by a record-studio
employee. Second, Cohen could not quite get the lyrics right. This last
line in his most famous stanza was added ten years after he began writing the song:

*Ring the bells that still can ring
Forget your perfect offering
There is a crack, a crack in everything
That's how the light gets in.*

For each of us, what we imagine as our most perfect lives or perfect circumstances, will eventually crack. Some day, they might even shatter. But that is how the light gets in.

As I drove away from that historic adobe chapel, the sun was setting over a pair of twin mesas in the distance. The sky had erupted into an exquisite array of yellow, orange, and peach light cascading from the horizon to the heavens. It felt as if my entire world was glowing. As if after five years in the dark, the light was finally getting in.

I was overflowing with a belief in God and overwhelmed by the grace that surrounds us each day. For me, the agony of uncertainty and the real and present danger of mortality cannot be navigated by a light spirituality or a vague nod to a higher power. To truly bear the excruciating unknown, I had found the most important ingredient for me to mix the golden glue that could repair my life, was simply *faith*. It was to have and to hold the certainty there is a God who is present with me always—in the light and, more importantly, in the dark.

I left Chimayo cradling my Holy Cup of Dixie, believing without a doubt, that my new book wasn't about dying. It was a story about this miracle of living.

16

BEING

EMBRACING RADICAL
UNCERTAINTY

Our battle living with rare disease has been exactly as Dr. Jane told us it would be—finding a way to live in faith not fear. Whether it is a disease, a death, or a divorce, something will shatter the safe life we carefully construct foolishly believing we are in control. That is the journey for each of us. In life, we cannot escape the fact that there will be suffering that will bring us to our knees. When it happens, we must find a way not only to rise, but learn to remain standing.

Dr. Rana Awdish understands death and suffering as both a patient and a physician. As the director of the Pulmonary Hypertension Program at Henry Ford Hospital in Detroit and a practicing critical care physician, Dr. Awdish has seen her share of trauma. It wasn't until she herself ended up in the emergency room and spent months fighting for her life after multiple organ failures, that she gained a new understanding of medicine and her own role as a doctor.

In her memoir, *In Shock: My Journey from Death to Recovery and the Redemptive Power of Hope,* Dr. Awdish writes:

> *As physicians, we so often feel we aren't enough. We've seen too much.*
> *We know the disease is stronger than the cure, we feel the deck is stacked*

and we can't possibly win. We frame our losses and successes in terms of the disease, which is a mistake. The language alone implies a battle and a clear outcome, a victor and a loser. If we are honest and allow ourselves to see death for what it is, an inescapable inevitability, then our story can change. In that light, we can accept that our greatest gift is not in healing, because all healing is transient. Our greatest gift is, in fact, our ability to be absolutely present with suffering. To allow it to transform us, and, by holding the suffering of others, transform it for them as well.

This transformation can easily get lost in the suffering. A disease like SCAD, or any other incurable condition, challenges our ability to live in wholehearted joy, yet healing is not only about finding a cure. For patients, healing is about finding a way for your soul to live with the radical uncertainties inherent in a difficult diagnosis, and with that discovery, the transformation begins. Charlie discovered his healing began on a river, finding peace with less sweat, less motion, and less muscle. And through the love of a dog who seemed to have a direct line to the divine. Finally, his transformation included retiring to discover next chapters and choosing what mattered most.

For caregivers, healing is about understanding that anxiety and grief are the price of love. Being present with suffering means accepting that we cannot control losing that love. To prevent the premature death of my own spirit, I had to learn to trust that I could survive in a life without Charlie. It meant finding a therapist, learning to ground myself through walking, discovering new sanctuaries, and rediscovering what was holy. To me, finding holy involved two pilgrimages: one traveling a sacred path and one seeking a sacred place. Together, those sacred journeys finally helped me develop a true faith. One where I could know with certainty that God is not simply hovering in the heavens but is beside us on this earth, in the light and the dark.

That is the real revelation. To believe there is divine grace woven in both miracles that astound us as well as miseries that break us. It is this shattering that will transform us.

There remains no cure for Spontaneous Coronary Artery Dissection. No life-saving pill or promising prognosis. There are hundreds of other diagnoses and many of life's most painful events that share this same truth. There is no way to fully recover from the death of a child or spouse, whether from disease, accident, or violence. After such a loss, we will not go back to who we were. Inevitably, when two hearts are bound by love, when one stops beating, the other will break. For this, there will never be a cure. All love carries this same risk. Once someone captures our heart, we are forever changed.

Each of Charlie's multiple diagnoses and multiple near-death traumas felt like cruel collisions. But in fact, with each emergency came a resurrection of our lives. After our first crisis and each one that followed, we were forced to dissect and discern how we wanted to live. To pull apart what mattered and what didn't. To value choices over obligations. To shift from moment-by-moment terror to moment-by-moment joy.

Through all life's fears and uncertainties, we are, as Reverend Lisa Saunders assured me, living under a canopy of blessings and grace. Each one of us has the choice to breathe in the beauty of every day. As we bear the unbearable—unwanted diagnosis, untimely deaths, unfair outcomes—we begin to understand that it takes surviving such a grief to comprehend a corresponding blessing. No opposite joy without the matching despair. We cannot fully fathom exuberance if we have never suffered anguish. We cannot live in full gratitude of this waking moment if we have never fully contemplated the loss of it.

I cannot explain how Charlie, with two rare diseases and three near-fatal events, remains wholly alive today. Whether through the trinity of exceptional medical team, the many prayers for healing, or his own incredible will to live, whatever the combination, his unlikely survival remains a medical mystery to me.

In her book *The Will to Live and Other Mysteries*, Dr. Rachel Naomi Remen writes:

> *As a person who has been a physician for 37 years, I have seen without a doubt that it is possible to study life for many years without knowing life and its power at all. Science will define life in its own way but life is larger than science. Things happen that science can't explain. These things are not replicable nor are they measurable. These things are touching, moving, inspiring, powerful. In my work with people with life-threatening illness and cancer, I have watched many people confront the unknown and even face death. In that confrontation with the unknown, I have watched them recover from a sense of numbness or cynicism. I have watched them become truly alive. It's almost as if they have remembered that life is holy, that to live is a blessing and they have reminded me as well.*

For many years, I believed that those sixty minutes in a New England café sharing turkey sandwiches before our wild ambulance ride marked our last ordinary hour on the worst day of our lives. I believed that because it was the last blissful hour, I could remember not worrying Charlie might die. I separated time into the Before and After. As I struggled to understand what was happening to us, I relegated all time after Charlie's heart attack as tainted, horrific hours mired in fear—which at that time, was true. Today, I see it differently.

The truth is, there are no ordinary hours. Each breath is sacred and each hour is a gift.

The day that began innocently in a café was not about death, it was about rebirth. Not only because Charlie lived but because it allowed us to see the world through a new lens of gratitude for all that is precious and sacred. To shake off our slumber of certainty. To begin to wake up to the fact that we are here with people we love in places we cherish for an undeterminable length of time. Which makes every minute, even the mundane, holy.

After living in constant fear of death every minute for years, this is what I can tell you about striving to be alive.

Fill your minutes with the music of life.
Fill your hours with pursuits that will matter.
Fill your days with loving others.
Fill your soul with all that is holy along the way.

Start small in your faith and then, keep digging deeper until you discover a peace with all the pieces that are yours to uncover. A shattered life can be made strong and beautiful again.

It's been seven years since Charlie collapsed on a hotel bed and I rushed him to an urgent care. Seven years since an ambulance delivered us to an emergency room where we discovered how fragile life can be. Seven years since we learned that a beating heart is truly a moment-by-moment miracle.

I never thought we would exhale from that day. I never thought I would stop watching Charlie's chest go up and down as he slept. But I no longer lie awake at night on high alert for Charlie's last breath. I go to sleep each evening whispering a resounding prayer of thanks for another day. Hundreds of days and counting since I first believed it was Charlie's last.

There is still both shock and wonder at what happened to us. The cardiac crash that ended all complacency in living. The everyday terror of fragile arteries that plagued us for years. The certainty that miracles occurred at least three times over to allow Charlie to live. All of that was part of the transformative process to let go of dying to begin living.

I wasted so many days asking the unanswerable question. *What if Charlie dies?* Mired in the fear of the unfathomable, I exhausted all energy and all possibility for the real question we both should have been asking: *What if Charlie lives?*

It is with enormous gratitude I write that as of today, I am still here on this earth with Charlie and each of our daughters, and, even now, a son-in-law who has expanded the love of our family. I fully understand that tomorrow, I could become a widow. By turn, after all this worry about Charlie's life, he could be attending my funeral before that dreaded day arrives when reason tells me, I must attend his. I control none of this. My choice remains only how I will live today.

While death is certain, life is the open-ended question. We have no assurance as to how long we will live but we absolutely receive the choice of how we spend our time. At our highest and best use, we can choose to spend each moment of each day in each year with people we love in pursuits we hope might transform our human experience. It is our choice whether we decide to live small and tight governed by fear or open and joyously grounded in full receipt of the gift that we are present together today. Maybe not tomorrow, but today.

Poet Rainer Maria Rilke wrote:

I want to ask you, as clearly as I can, to bear with patience all that is unresolved in your heart, and try to love the questions themselves. . . . For everything must be lived. Live the questions now, perhaps then, someday, you will gradually, without noticing, live into the answer.

It has taken all my life to gain this perspective. To be patient with all that is unresolved. To concede what little control we have in our lives. To embrace radical uncertainty. My choice has become to live each moment so that they begin to add up to a day, a month, a year, and finally, a life worthy of this single, miraculous chance I have been given. Just as Poppop spent twelve years mastering his questions, I want to know mine. With each remaining day, I hope to live with such intention that when I know enough to ask my final question, I will have lived into my one remaining, wondrous answer.

EPILOGUE

The last pages of this book were finished in the fall of 2019, six months before the COVID-19 pandemic would change the world. Six months before everyone would learn a new way of living and we would need to stay apart to stay alive.

During those shelter-in-place days, I had all the time I needed to write, yet I resisted sitting down to make the final edits to this book. In its present form, it was a "happy" ending. Charlie lives into a new chapter. I write my way into living in faith not fear. With all my heart, I wanted that ending to stand. But Charlie had three risk factors for COVID-19: compromised heart, weakened lungs, and a sixty-year-old body. I was plagued by the thought that there was a new ending and another new chapter that I didn't want to write.

So we were beyond careful. We could go days without seeing another human except each other. We made video-chat dates with our daughters, family, and friends. We wore masks and gloves and used hand sanitizer with a dedicated fervor. Later that same COVID summer, we moved part-time to the mountains of Wyoming to live out the dream I always had for us after Charlie's retirement—two, wrinkly, gray-haired, soul mates growing old, fly-fishing on a trout-filled river.

I had no idea that the lessons I had learned over the last seven years would be exactly the skills I would need to live through each long day of a corona-virus-threatened world. I began each morning writing, and then grounding myself in long walks in forests, which helped me release old ideas that we could ever predict what disease might be our most mortal threat. I was once again on a new labyrinth path of life, learning to Release, Receive, and Return from this new COVID journey and hoping to have gained some wisdom from the experience.

Unlike the freshly terrifying SCAD nights where I wrestled with worry that I might wake to become a widow, I slept fairly peacefully during that long pandemic-threatened year. Surviving seven years of worry about sudden-splitting arteries and fatal heart attacks still seemed far more terrifying than the virus that was reordering our planet as well as our own home.

It's not that I did not worry one of us might wake one day with a fever that would match the horrible reality we watched each day on the twenty-four-hour news cycle. I did in fact pray each morning upon waking and each night before sleeping, not only for the health of so many I loved, but also for the healthcare workers who might need to heal them. I had come to rest in the trust of a divine plan I could not possibly fathom.

The real lesson, which I had already learned well, was how little we can control. I had already realized how gratitude for the present day can lessen the anxiety of the unknown future. I had already come to believe in the God who comforts even in despair. It was stunning to witness the entire country forced into individual spiritual cocoons and imagine what transformations might be spinning inside.

The blue lights that lit the night in gratitude for our healers. The mosaic of musicians on videos reminding us how notes can make our spirits soar. The millions who rallied to help their neighbors with masks or groceries or sidewalk-chalk messages of love. Even as thousands of lives were tragically lost, it seemed millions more were holy found.

Imagine what might ultimately emerge from this frightening time. A people more interested in helping each other rather than harming each other. A country united by what is joining us rather than what is dividing us. A family of nations willing to remember our fates are inextricably bound together.

Maybe that was the worldwide lesson of 2020. Together, in unison, we all experienced our last ordinary hour.

May we all rediscover the wonder in our lives, recognize the holy in our every day, and remember—always—that there is no such thing as an ordinary hour.

ACKNOWLEDGMENTS

There were many drafts over many years before this writing project became a book. It would have been impossible to live this story without all the friends and family who surrounded us and lifted us up. While the stories of dinners, lunches, and long walks were not told on these pages, they were very much a part of our healing. Charlie and I are incredibly lucky to have not only extraordinary family but friends we count as family as well. Since this story spanned seven years, to name each remarkable act of kindness would risk leaving one out. So I say a very inadequate but deeply felt *Thank you* to the many who have walked this walk with us and know much more than the details recounted here. Especially my Grace Group, the Lunch Group, my Phil sisters, the Schpilkies, and the new Angel whisperers who give me courage.

For Charlie's continued health, there are as my family says, "no words" to thank the countless healthcare heroes we may never know the names of who have helped us at Atrium Health and Novant Health in Charlotte, Lowell General Hospital in Massachusetts, and Mayo Clinic in Rochester, Minnesota. But we are grateful every day for:

Dr. Jane Harrell and Dr. Josh Shoemake
   and their incredible team at H3 Healthcare

Dr. Sharonne Hayes

Dr. Craig Daniels

Dr. Zvonimir Milas

Dr. Geoffrey A. Rose

and Katherine Leon who isn't a physician, but after all the SCAD survivors she has helped, deserves an honorary medical degree.

For this book, there are so many who bring a manuscript to life. But special thanks to:

Edwina Willis Fleming for believing in this book before I did.

Tammie Lesesne for guiding me through the roughest waters.

Heidi Rotberg, PhD, for walking beside me in the dark and showing me a way out.

Meg Robertson for coaching me to dream bigger and believe anything is possible.

Reverend Lisa Saunders for always giving me the right words.

Margaret Wrinkle for helping me envision the first pages and encouraging first drafts.

Kate Radamacher for the Wild Goose way we met and for becoming my first author friend.

Niki Hardy for asking questions that led to deeper drafts.

My Mastermind and HopeCircle women who cheered me on.

Brian Allain for introductions and inspiration.

Kathy Helmers for the brilliant suggestion to begin again and giving me confidence.

Leighton and Jeanie Ford for their listening, mentoring and modeling what love should be. I could go "three times around the world" and never witness a better example.

Beta readers:

Sarah Belk, Tricia Bernard, Nancy Engen, Leslie Hooton, Susan Izard, Jean Izard, and Julie Marr. And especially Truth Teller, Carrie Banwell, who gave me just the right way to begin and Kristin Hills Bradberry who gave me just the right the way to end.

Elizabeth Dickens for polishing this manuscript with her incredible eye for editing. I will be always grateful for the dad nudges that brought us together.

Debra Nichols for sharp eyes to make these pages perfect and being much more than a proofreader.

Karen Minster for the interior design to make these pages perfectly beautiful and once again making it possible to put my words in the world.

Jon Valk for the most beautiful and inspirational cover I loved at first sight.

And always and ever,
Charlie, Lauren, Kailey, Maddie, Emma, and now, Pete
—this circle of seven is my heart.

READING & LISTENING

This is a complete list of the authors, books, articles, and podcasts referred to in each chapter.

SHATTERING

READ: Dr. Rana Awdish, *In Shock: My Journey from Death to Recovery and the Redemptive Power of Hope* (Picador; October 2018)

1. BREAKING: The Moment We Never See Coming

READ: Dr. Elisabeth Kübler-Ross, *On Death and Dying: What the Dying Have to Teach Doctors, Nurses, Clergy, and Their Own Families* (Scribner; Reissue edition, August 2014)

2. REELING: Leaving Who We Were

LISTEN: *On Being with Krista Tippett.* Episode: Dr. Rachel Naomi Remen, *The Difference between Curing and Healing* (original airdate August 11, 2005), https://onbeing.org/programs/rachel-naomi -remen-the-difference-between-fixing-and-healing-nov2018/

READ: Dr. Rachel Naomi Remen, *Kitchen Table Wisdom: Stories that Heal* (Riverhead Books; Tenth Anniversary edition, August 1, 2006)

READ: David Whyte, *Consolations: The Solace, Nourishment and Underlying Meaning of Everyday Words* (Many Rivers Press; First edition, January 1, 2015)

LISTEN: David Whyte, *Thresholds: Navigating the Difficult Transitions of Life* (Many Rivers Press; Audio CD, December 1, 2002)

3. COPING: Medical Emergencies Lead to Spiritual Emergencies

READ: Richard Rohr, *Falling Upward: A Spirituality for the Two Halves of Life* (Jossey-Bass; First edition, April 19, 2011)

READ: Barbara Brown Taylor, *An Altar in the World: A Geography of Faith* (HarperOne; Reprint edition, February 9, 2010)

READ: Barbara Brown Taylor, *Learning to Walk in the Dark* (HarperOne; Reprint edition, March 24, 2015)

4. FALLING: When Bad News Becomes Worse News

READ: Laurie Goodstein, "Reviving Labyrinths, Paths to Inner Peace" *The New York Times,* May 10, 1998, https://www.nytimes.com /1998/05/10/us/reviving-labyrinths-paths-to-inner-peace.html

READ: Reverend Lauren Artress, *Walking a Sacred Path, Rediscovering the Labyrinth as a Spiritual Practice* (Riverhead Books; Revised edition, March 7, 2006)

RELEASING

5. SEEKING: Answers Already Waiting to Be Found

READ: Malin Dollinger, M.D., and Bernard Dubrow, M.S., "Living with Mortality: Life Goes On," Stanford Medicine, https://med.stanford.edu/survivingcancer/cancers-existential -questions/cancer-living-mortality-fear.html

READ: Frederick Buechner, *Listening to Your Life: Daily Meditations with Frederick Buechner* (HarperOne; First edition, May 8, 1992)

6. CONNECTING: The Current of Grace Healing Us All

READ: Dr. Elisabeth Kübler-Ross, and David Kessler, *On Grief and Grieving: Finding the Meaning of Grief Through the Five Stages of Loss* (Scribner; First edition, August 2014)

READ: Morgan Manella, "90% of Americans have prayed for healing, study finds" (CNN.com, April 25, 2016), https://www.cnn.com/2016/04/25/health/healing-power-of-prayer-study/index.html

READ: Dr. Joanne Cacciatore, *Bearing the Unbearable: Love, Loss, and the Heartbreaking Path of Grief* (Wisdom Publications; First edition, June 27, 2017)

READ: Rachel Held Evans, *Searching for Sunday: Loving, Leaving, and Finding the Church* (Thomas Nelson Books; April 14, 2015)

7. AWAKENING: The Choice to Live in Faith Not Fear

READ: Harvard Health Publishing, "Sour mood getting you down? Get back to nature," (July 2018), https://www.health.harvard.edu/mind-and-mood/sour-mood-getting-you-down-get-back-to-nature

READ: L. R. Knost, *Two Thousand Kisses a Day: Gentle Parenting Through the Ages and Stages* (Little Hearts Books, LLC; February 2013)

8. LEARNING: The Shift from Chronos Time to Kairos Time

READ: Sue Monk Kidd, *When the Heart Waits: Spiritual Direction for Life's Sacred Questions* (HarperOne; October 11, 2016)

RECEIVING

9. GROUNDING: We Make the Way by Walking

WATCH: *The Way* (2010, movie)

READ: Bruce Feiler, "The New Allure of Sacred Pilgrimages" (The New York Times, December 20, 2014), https://www.nytimes.com/2014/12/21/sunday-review/the-new-allure-of-sacred-pilgrimages.html

READ: Antonio Machado, *There is No Road: Proverbs by Antonio Machado* (Series: *Companions for the Journey*, White Pine Press; First edition, September 1, 2003)

10. SPIRALING: The Discovery of How Strong We Can Become

READ: Glennon Doyle Melton, *Untamed* (The Dial Press; March 10, 2020)

11. REVIVING: Each Day Is a Holy Place

READ: Sarah Bessey, *Miracles and Other Reasonable Things: A Story of Unlearning and Relearning God* (Howard Books; October 8, 2019)

READ: Sarah Bessey, *A Prayer for the Brokenhearted at Christmas*, https://sarahbessey.com/essays/broken-hearted-christmas

READ: John O'Donohue, *To Bless the Space Between Us: A Book of Blessings* (Doubleday; First edition, March 4, 2008)

12. BELIEVING: Under a Canopy of Blessings and Grace

READ: Dr. Lee Warren, *I've Seen the End of You: A Neurosurgeon's Look at Faith, Doubt, and the Things We Think We Know* (WaterBrook Press; January 7, 2020)

READ: Reverend Lisa G. Saunders, *Even at the Grave* (Mill City Press, Inc.; November 28, 2017)

RETURNING

13. CHOOSING: Finding What Matters in This World

READ: David Brooks, *The Second Mountain: The Quest for a Moral Life* (Random House; April 16, 2019)

READ: Dr. Robert M. Sapolsky, *Why Zebras Don't Get Ulcers* (Holt Paperbacks; Third edition, September 15, 2004)

READ: Thomas Merton, *The Seven Storey Mountain: An Autobiography of Faith* (Mariner Books; First edition, October 4, 1999)

READ: John O'Donohue, *To Bless the Space Between Us: A Book of Blessings* (Doubleday; First edition, March 4, 2008)

14. LOVING: Lessons from a Widow

READ: Dr. Sunita Puri, *That Good Night: Life and Medicine in the Eleventh Hour* (Penguin Books; Reprint edition, March 3, 2020)

READ: Enuma Okoro, *Reluctant Pilgrim: A Moody, Somewhat Self-Indulgent Introvert's Search for Spiritual Community* (Fresh Air Books; First edition, October 1, 2010)

READ: Margaret Wrinkle, *Wash* (Atlantic Monthly Press; First edition, February 5, 2013)

READ: Jan Richardson, *The Cure for Sorrow: A Book of Blessings for Times of Grief* (Wanton Gospeller Press; November 15, 2016)

15. HEALING: Prayers for Acceptance

READ: Dr. Mary C. Neal, *7 Lessons from Heaven: How Dying Taught Me to Live a Joy-Filled Life* (Convergent Books; September 19, 2017)

READ: Dr. Kate C. Bowler, *Everything Happens for a Reason (and Other Lies I've Loved)* (Random House; June 4, 2019)

LISTEN: *Everything Happens, A Podcast with Kate Bowler,* https://katebowler.com/podcasts/

16. BEING: Embracing Radical Uncertainty

READ: Dr. Rana Awdish, *In Shock: My Journey from Death to Recovery and the Redemptive Power of Hope* (Picador; October 2018)

LISTEN: Rachel Naomi Remen, *The Will to Live and Other Mysteries* (Sounds True; April 1, 2001)

Q & A WITH KATHY IZARD

1. How long did it take you to write *The Last Ordinary Hour,* and what was your process?

The first pages of this book which began "If I had to pick a moment, one moment . . ." poured out one day while I was curled up writing and Charlie was fishing. It was February 2018—the five-year anniversary of Charlie's initial SCAD. After five years, I guess my soul decided it was time to bring everything into the light. I never expected to write about this part of my life because for so long, it was just too dark a chapter. It was my friend, Edwina Willis Fleming, who said one day, "This is going to help so many people."

I could not imagine why she thought that or how I might be able to write about it. But the first three chapters poured out in one sitting, yet I still put them away for three months until that Santa Fe writing workshop with Margaret Wrinkle. She is an amazing teacher and much of the last three chapters arrived as a result of her class. From there, I had to figure out how to bridge what I had written—from the turkey sandwiches in the café in New England to the chapel in Chimayo, New Mexico. From start to finish this manuscript encompassed three years and eighteen versions. At first, I wrote it as pure memoir—just a timeline of all that happened. Margaret was my book coach for that version and I still have that draft only for my family.

I thought I was finished with a final draft of this memoir in February of 2020. Exactly one month before a global pandemic changed the whole world. At the time, I had no idea that the lessons I had learned over the last seven years would be exactly the same skills I would need to live through our quarantined world. The real lesson was, I had learned already: we are not in control. I understood how gratitude for the present day can lessen the anxiety of a radically unknown future.

It was Kathy Helmers who asked me to consider looking at my draft a little differently. What if I wrote the book not only about my story but the process that helped me evolve my thinking from fear to faith? What would that version look like?

So, I dismantled my carefully crafted book and began again. As written, it would not have been very helpful. There was no implicit guidance to help people on their journeys through fear and I hadn't woven in all the books I had read written by master teachers who helped me navigate my new reality living with a medical death sentence. Beyond my story, I needed to tell readers about some of the stories that ultimately helped me rewrite my own. It was only upon writing and reflection that I could see how our cardiac crash had resulted in a resurrection which allowed both Charlie and me to begin living our best lives.

This final edition became version 18.1111 and it is my revised book of not only of what happened, but more importantly, how I learned to move through it, which I hope will help you move through whatever you are facing. How I stopped expecting the worst to happen and began waking up to the wonder in my life. How I am no longer waiting for some day in the future to begin living. How I will never again take for granted the fact that either Charlie or I woke up today.

2. How did Charlie feel about you writing about him?

When I was writing this over the first two years, I did not let anyone read it. I am not sure if I believed I was brave enough to put this story into the world or that Charlie would want me to. He is intensely private, so having his health history as public record was pretty radical for him. He doesn't even have any social media accounts because he doesn't want anyone knowing anything about him! So this book would be a huge stretch. But he read the very personal, original version I've kept for our family. He read it in one sitting and when he finished, he just gave me a long hug. I think it was pretty overwhelming for him to read because much of it he doesn't remember. I think that is the difficult part for patients and caregivers—our experiences are the same but different. While he might remember the physical pain and the procedures, I remember the fear and the uncertainty. I half expected him to say he couldn't let me put that much of him in the story. But he didn't. He was 100% supportive. I think maybe having this story written down helps him feel less "crazy." All that happened to him was, frankly, unbelievable, so once he saw it all written down, it helped us both. When all the stories of SCAD and Code Blue are put together, we understood why we both felt, and still feel, like he might die at any minute.

3. How do you explain that after so many close calls and even the "R on T phenomenon," that Charlie is still alive?

I really can't. I guess that is why I needed to write this book. It defies belief that a guy with two rare diseases and three near misses is still here. Like the woman in my writer's workshop said, "I thought it was fiction and I didn't buy it." It is the truth but I cannot say why the logical outcome has not yet happened. I think about Dr. Jane telling Charlie, "You should be dead three times over. You need to find out why God still wants you here." So he is. We both are.

4. That begs the question, if and when Charlie dies will you be angry with God? Will it change your faith?

I can't know how I will feel when that day comes, but I hope I won't lose faith when it does. I think ten years ago that might have been true— that I could become angry and dwell in bitterness. But so much has happened not only with my faith but with our family. I am so grateful that Charlie has made it to see each of the girls graduate from high school, college, and now even graduate school. In 2019, we had our first wedding and we are sharing the joy of seeing each of the girls blossom into who they were meant to be. Charlie is here to witness all of that. When he survived his first SCAD, Maddie and Emma were seniors in high school—such a very different time. Right now, I am just grateful. So grateful that we have had so much more time together than we would have if that first heart attack took his life. Would I like to be guaranteed that we grow old together? Absolutely. But I don't believe it changes the miracles in our story or my faith.

5. What would you say to readers who are going through their own struggles with a rare disease or who have already lost that spouse or child?

I can't begin to know what they are going through or that ultimate pain. When they called the Code Blue on Charlie and the priest came, I got the dress rehearsal and it was horrific. So first I would say, I am sorry. Grief is all-consuming and something I believe is ahead for me. While it is possible I will predecease Charlie, logic tells me that I will be left here and he will—someday—die first. I have, however, spent more than the average amount of time thinking and reading about that eventual outcome. The extensive reading list at the back of this book includes resources I have found to be enormously helpful and comforting. I hope they can be a starting place for anyone who is struggling with their own crisis and help bring a measure of peace.

6. This book is different from your first memoir, *The Hundred Story Home,* and maybe not what readers expected. Did you expect this would be your sequel?

Not at all! As I said, I never imagined writing this, and frankly, never imagined living it!

The timeline was really interesting because Charlie's first heart attack happened one year after Moore Place opened. Three years into our SCAD life, I published *The Hundred Story Home* and began speaking about that experience. While I was talking publicly about homelessness and mental health, I was not talking about rare diseases and the havoc it was wreaking in our life behind the scenes. I know readers probably expected my next book to be a follow-up to the Moore Place stories, but this had to come first. I realized that meeting Denver Moore and the shift my life took as a result was the first half of my faith journey. This experience with Charlie, this was the deeper, second half of my faith journey. Everything I believe going forward is a result of living these past seven years worrying about imminent death. But it has taught me there are things worse than dying and among them, living as if you already are. If we don't remember that every moment is holy and every day a gift, then we are not really alive.

7. Are you working on your next book and can you tell us what that is about?

Now that I have written this second half of my faith journey in *The Last Ordinary Hour*, I am returning to the continuing miracles that are playing out as a result of the work I did with Moore Place and HopeWay. I have been collecting stories that record the grace in everyday life. For a while, I have been calling them the "God Dots" in my life. I have decided to trust my newest whisper to write these stories down, connecting the God Dots so I won't be the only one to bear witness. This book will be about the series of God Dots that I follow or that follow me. Stories that need to be remembered and stories that need to be told. Once I began collecting them, it seemed the more stories there were to tell. Once I was paying attention, I realized the magic was all around me, just waiting to be found.

READER'S GUIDE FOR
BOOK CLUBS AND STUDY GROUPS

Thank you for reading *The Last Ordinary Hour*. Here are some questions to get the conversation started for your book club or study group. If you have discussed *The Last Ordinary Hour* or read *The Hundred Story Home* let us know. We love to hear what resonates with your group in this guide or the themes that you discussed. Send your comments and suggestions to womenfaithstory@gmail.com

1. One of the central themes in this book is rare disease and how it affects both caregiver and patient. While this story is told from the caregiver's point of view, Charlie, the patient experienced the story very differently. What were some of the differences in dealing with a rare disease through the caregiver's and patient's perspectives?

2. Have you had to navigate a chronic condition, illness, or rare disease as either a patient or caregiver? How did you find it different to navigate as the one undergoing treatment versus caretaking? What were the stress points between you and the patient or caregiver?

3. *The Last Ordinary Hour* is written in four sections: Shattering, Releasing, Receiving, and Returning. These sections are designed to mirror the process that Kathy felt she experienced on her journey of dealing with a rare disease and coming to terms with living with it. Have you or a friend experienced something that felt like the first stage—Shattering? What were some of the steps you took to recover?

4. The process of Kintsugi is referenced in Chapter 1 as well as on the cover design. Kathy tells us: "In Japan, there is an ancient art of Kintsugi—repairing broken pottery by filling the cracks with gold. Practitioners of this 400-year-old technique believe these imperfect yet restored pieces are even more beautiful once made whole again." And then asks, "How do we discover the gold to bind our broken selves?" How do you see Kathy searching for the gold to repair her life? Have you found similar processes in order to heal after a devastating crisis?

5. The labyrinth is used as a metaphor throughout the story based on the work by the Reverend Lauren Artress and her experiential three-part process: Releasing, Receiving, Returning. Have you ever learned about labyrinths before or walked one yourself? What was your experience?

6. In Chapter 2, Kathy uses the work of David Whyte to discuss "doors you don't want to go through." In the book, Kathy eventually crosses many thresholds and has at least one other pivotal moment regarding doors. Discuss this metaphor of thresholds in our lives and what some have been for you.

7. More than thirty-five authors, poets, theologians, and doctors are referenced in *The Last Ordinary Hour*. In Chapter 3, Kathy writes, "I no longer wanted to be distracted when I read—I wanted to be fed." How does this resonate with you? Why do you read? Which of the quotes or ideas referenced by other authors throughout the book were most impactful to you and why?

8. In the book, Charlie and Kathy experience a continuing series of medical crises that force them to begin navigating their world differently. What were some of the choices they made and how did their

different roles (caregiver vs. patient) dictate those choices? Have you had to navigate similar choices? How did you decide to live differently?

9. Chapter 5 is titled "Seeking" with the subtitle: "Answers Already Waiting to Be Found." In this chapter, Kathy writes about her father-in-law's (Poppop) study through EfM and a twelve-year quest for an answer to one last question. Throughout the book, Kathy is on a similar quest for faith. Have you wrestled with your faith in some way? What are the questions you struggle with and how do you search for answers?

10. In Chapter 8, Kathy writes about learning about *Chronos* vs. *Kairos* time. This concept is central to making a shift from minute-by-minute worry to moment-by-moment joy. Have you ever studied this perception of time? How might it help you deal with difficult circumstances in your life?

11. "Grounding," the idea of walking and connecting to nature as a spiritual practice, is a recurring theme. Kathy eventually walks a section of the Camino that becomes a powerful experience in her life. There is also symbol of the Camino on this book cover. Chapter 9 also references the idea of embarking on sacred journeys and the "330 million people who travel annually as part of a pilgrimage." Have you ever taken part in a type of pilgrimage or sacred journey? What was your experience?

12. After walking the Camino, Kathy felt solid in her faith and believed she was ready to navigate her new world. Soon after, however, there were two more difficult medical emergencies that tested her faith once again. She describes "ranting and railing" at the priest who arrived after the Code Blue emergency. Has your faith ever been tested? How did you react? Were you able to recover your faith or has it remained shaken? If you were tested in some way, how did your faith deepen after?

13. In searching for meaning, Kathy writes in Chapter 12 about meeting with an Episcopal priest, the Reverend Lisa Saunders, who reframes her thinking with the idea of "a canopy of blessings and grace." Where do you see the idea of blessings and grace throughout this story? Where do you see a canopy of blessings and grace in your own life?

14. Throughout the book, Kathy is terrified about becoming a widow. In Chapter 14, she meets Maria who is already a widow. Maria found comfort in defining spirituality with her husband before he died. What do you believe gave her comfort, and how did that help her survive his death? How might defining your spirituality help you navigate loss?

15. Kathy describes her fear about writing an "ending she did not want to write." At the end of this book, Charlie is still alive despite living with two rare diseases and three nearly fatal experiences. While he is not cured, Kathy writes that she believes "they have both been healed." In what ways do you see evidence of this healing? What choices were made to facilitate this healing?

16. While the "Shattering," is the beginning of this story, the transformation is the ending. Kathy writes:

"That is the real revelation. To believe there is divine grace woven in both miracles that astound us as well as miseries that break us. It is this shattering that will transform us."

What has "shattered" you? How have you been transformed? And if you are still shattered, how might you begin to seek transformation?

17. In the beginning, Kathy believes "the last ordinary hour" is the time before she knew about SCAD and that Charlie could die at any moment. Kathy writes:

"I relegated all time after Charlie's heart attack as tainted, horrific hours mired in fear—which at that time, was true. Today, I see it differently.

The truth is, there are no ordinary hours. Each breath is sacred and each hour is a gift.

The day that began innocently in a café was not about death, it was about rebirth. Not only because Charlie lived but because it allowed us to see the world through a new lens of gratitude for all that is precious and sacred. To shake off our slumber of certainty. To begin to wake up to the fact that we are here with people we love in places we cherish for an undeterminable length of time. Which makes every minute, even the mundane, holy."

After reading, how has this book made you see your life differently? How might you make choices that will help you live as if every minute is holy?

SPONTANEOUS CORONARY ARTERY DISSECTION (SCAD)

By Katherine Leon

SCAD Survivor, Co-Founder and Board Chair, SCAD Alliance

As you read Kathy Izard's vivid descriptions in each chapter, you most likely felt the hopelessness and pain SCAD can cause patients, our families, and even our healthcare teams. The complexity of this devastating disease is what motivated survivors Rachel Doucette and me to create a nonprofit in 2013 called SCAD Alliance to support, educate, and find answers through research. We invite you to learn more about SCAD Alliance in this section.

The mission of SCAD Alliance is to be the leader in advancing the science of SCAD through improved knowledge and cooperation among healthcare professionals, patients, and their families. We pursue this mission by educating key audiences and fostering unique, interdisciplinary research collaborations. Our primary programs are education and professional awareness, patient support, and advancing research through the independent, multicenter iSCAD Registry.

This Q&A was prepared by the SCAD Alliance Scientific Advisory Board. The link to the full document, "Answers Especially for You," follows.

What exactly is SCAD? Is it a heart attack?

Spontaneous Coronary Artery Dissection (SCAD) is an under-diagnosed cause of acute coronary syndrome, heart attack, and sudden cardiac arrest. SCAD occurs when the inner layer of an artery tears or splits and allows blood to seep into the adjacent layer. The blood either pools (forming a blockage or hematoma), or the dissection continues to tear, creating a flap of tissue that blocks blood flow in the artery.

The artery involved and severity of blockage is what determines whether SCAD causes acute coronary syndrome (e.g., angina), a heart attack with muscle damage [called a STEMI or ST-segment elevation myocardial infarction (MI) as shown by changes on an electrocardiogram (ECG or EKG)], a heart attack without muscle damage (a non-STEMI, when the artery is partially blocked), or sudden cardiac arrest.

How do I know if I'm experiencing SCAD?

Although there are no tests to predict a dissection, it is vital to pay attention to your body's cues. The warning signs of SCAD are the symptoms of a heart attack: chest pain or pressure, jaw pain, extreme fatigue, shortness of breath, arm pain, clammy sweating, lightheadedness, and nausea.

Some SCAD patients report a sharp, sudden pain, which may have signaled their dissection. Others develop several vague symptoms over time, such as fatigue, lightheadedness and chest pressure, before finally experiencing the "classic" heart attack. Still others report having very mild symptoms, such as arm pain or tingling.

Emergency medical care for these symptoms is critical. If the sensation you're experiencing is "not right" for you, seek care immediately, particularly if you have recently given birth or participated in a similarly stressful exertion. Nearly 15% of all female SCAD patients are in the peripartum period (the last trimester or in the weeks after having a baby). Males and other female SCAD survivors report symptoms follow after unusual stress or participation in an extreme workout.

What is the right way to treat SCAD?

Because each patient is unique, there is no right or wrong way to treat SCAD; however, early research suggests that a conservative approach may be best for the majority of patients. The most conservative approach is to use medication to thin the blood, prevent clots, control blood pressure, and help the heart pump more easily so that the dissection can heal. This is generally called "medication management" or "medically managed" SCAD.

In other cases, the cardiologist may choose percutaneous coronary intervention (PCI) to open up the blocked area using stents, which are tiny, metal mesh tubes that act as scaffolding for the artery. A similar approach is to use balloon angioplasty to press open the blockage and restart flow. In either procedure, the cardiologist uses a catheter to access the blockage and place the stent (or deploy the balloon) through your artery. Threading a catheter through the artery may worsen an existing tear or create a new one, which is why experts advise against PCI if possible and suggest the medication management approach instead.

Some patients may require coronary artery bypass grafting (CABG, pronounced "cabbage" or called open heart surgery) to correct blockages in areas that cannot be safely stented or when the risk of heart muscle damage is great. In these cases, new pathways are created by rerouting blood flow around the dissection using the internal mammary artery or veins from the leg or arm.

Learn more about SCAD and patient concerns through this link: http://scadalliance.org/wp-content/uploads/2017/07/QA-web-doc -020416-low-final.pdf

MORE INFORMATION AND SUPPORT

SCAD Alliance website: https://scadalliance.org/

SCAD Alliance is a 501(c)3 nonprofit staffed by volunteers who are connected to SCAD either as a survivor, family member, friend, or dedicated physician. The SCAD Alliance vision is to empower each survivor with an accurate diagnosis, superior outcome, and answers. We host a variety of patient resources on our website and our social media pages including current SCAD articles and publications, and resources to connect patients to support opportunities, both in person and online. Our webinar series, "Ask the Experts," hosts monthly discussions with SCAD experts on a variety of topics as they relate to SCAD.

For details about SCAD, caregiver information, and to connect with SCAD Alliance, we offer the following resources:

SCAD Alliance website: https://scadalliance.org/
iSCAD Registry website: https://iscadregistry.bidmc.org/
facebook.com/SCADalliance
twitter.com/SCADalliance
youtube.com/SCADalliance

ADVANCING RESEARCH

SCAD Alliance launched the iSCAD Registry, a multicenter U.S. data repository and research initiative, in 2019. At the time of this publication, we have 16 sites nationwide with more than 525 patients enrolled and followed by the registry team. The iSCAD Registry is a robust collaboration designed to develop and maintain an independent, quality data source to advance the pace and breadth of SCAD research. The iSCAD Registry listing on the NIH Clinical Trials website, including participating sites and contacts, can be found at https://clinicaltrials.gov/ct2/show/NCT04496687

FOR MORE ON SCAD HEART ATTACKS

The following articles were recently written by leaders in the field of SCAD and provide a comprehensive overview of SCAD, related conditions, and considerations for the healthcare team:

Kim, Esther S. H., "Spontaneous Coronary-Artery Dissection." *N Engl J Med.* 2020; 383:2358-70. DOI: 10.1056/NEJMra2001524

Wood, Malissa J., "A Different Kind of Heart Attack." *Harvard Health Publishing;* 2019.

Hayes, Sharonne N., Kim, Esther S. H., Saw, Jacqueline, et al. "Spontaneous Coronary Artery Dissection: Current State of the Science: A Scientific Statement from the American Heart Association." Circulation; 2018; 137(19):e523-e557. doi:10.1161 /CIR.0000000000000564.

SANGER HEART & VASCULAR INSTITUTE

Kathy and Charlie Izard are proud to support the Atrium Health and Sanger Clinic partnership to create a new dedicated cardiovascular care center in Charlotte.

Building upon its fifty-year partnership with Atrium Health, Sanger Heart & Vascular Institute in Charlotte opened a state-of-the-art out-patient facility in 2021, bringing to life its vision that every patient is offered the clinical expertise and experience rivaling the best in the nation. Although certain aspects of cardiovascular (CV) care require delivery within hospital-based facilities, approximately 90% of CV care is now offered on an outpatient basis. To keep pace with this need and the projected growth of CV patients in the region, the new facility houses twelve centers of excellence that address various aspects of CV care; cardiac prevention and rehabilitation services, including a gym and culinary facility; and advanced imaging services—all under one roof, proximate to the main Carolinas Medical Center campus. The outpatient centers will be a driving force for innovations in education and research, integrating virtual access and remote patient monitoring capabilities, as well as closing gaps in care within underserved communities.

SPIRITUAL DIRECTION GUIDE

How to Begin
A NOTE FROM KATHY

When I began the first drafts of *The Last Ordinary Hour*, I wasn't clear exactly what this book might become. I knew Charlie's cardiac challenges started a process of transformation both in his body and in my soul. I looked at the world so differently after I learned how quickly everything could change. In order to live in radical uncertainly, I needed to find a faith that could allow me to wake up each day without the constant fear that it would be my first day as a widow. There were so many people who were a part of that transformation, including all the authors, podcasters, and theologians woven into these stories. My journey was circuitous, winding its way toward whole, and like Poppop, I imagine that I will be seeking answers until my last breath.

If after reading, you feel you need a spiritual direction guide for your journey, I have included one here. It is written by my oldest sister, the Reverend Louise Green who graduated from Harvard Divinity School. For three decades, Louise has been a leader in both ministry and social justice in Washington, DC. Since she has become a wise oracle in my life, I felt she was the perfect person to help readers who wanted to dig deeper into their own faith. The following guide is meant to be an interfaith approach to seeking connection with a higher spirit. I do believe everyone's path to understanding the divine is different. While some may find their true connection through traditional houses of faith, others might need a wider road to discover the path to their soul.

In *Now and Then: A Memoir of Vocation,* Frederick Buechner wrote:

"Listen to your life. See it for the fathomless mystery it is. In the boredom and pain of it, no less than in the excitement and gladness: touch, taste, smell your way to the holy and hidden heart of it, because in the last analysis all moments are key moments, and life itself is grace."

My deepest hope for *The Last Ordinary Hour* and the Spirit Journey which begins on the next page is that it helps you listen to your life and reconnects you to the holy all around you just waiting to be found.

SPIRIT JOURNEY

Designing Your Own Spiritual Practice
BY REVEREND LOUISE GREEN

STEP ONE: Assess reality. Decide to begin.

We keep trying to get away from the fundamental ambiguity of being human, and we can't.

We can't escape it any more than we can escape change, any more than we can escape death. The cause of our suffering is our reaction to the reality of no escape. . . .

We have a choice. We can spend our whole life suffering because we can't relax with how things really are, or we can relax and embrace the open-endedness of the human situation.

—PEMA CHÖDRÖN
Living Beautifully with Uncertainty and Change,
pp. 12–13

Most people start intentional spiritual practice in response to a deep yearning to live with less suffering, and more "relax-and-embrace" skill.

Because we all exist in the midst of constant change and challenge, we would do well to improve our navigation systems. If life is a series of waves, we can keep tumbling into the undertow, or choose to design a container headed where we prefer to go. At the least, we can build a better boat to provide more shelter when the waves hit hardest.

As we finally realize that life is going to remain ambiguous, we are often experiencing big change. Disruptive events impact our carefully constructed strategies, and the unraveling begins. Whether those disruptive situations are moderate meltdowns or major upheavals, it helps tremendously to cultivate practices that steady the spirit, focus the mind, and open the heart to deeper experience.

What is *spiritual practice,* anyway? I use this phrase in a particular pragmatic way. If you take music lessons or a dance class, move through a sports workout, or do a craft project, you know what practice means.

The word *spiritual* could simply mean bolstering your own inner spirit, or it could imply connecting to a transcendent Spirit with many names. Practice is a series of steps, done with purpose, repetition, and focus. Spiritual practice is not a special mystery, available only to people with religious professions and advanced faith credentials. It is all about mindful awareness and intention, over time.

There are really just a few key questions: **Do you want to do it? Why? When?** Most of us engage in plenty of drama around these queries employing procrastination, overplanning, overthinking, outright resistance, or subtle avoidance. Yet the essence of practice is simple: **do or don't do.**

In the group workshops or individual coaching work of *Spirit Journey* which I facilitate, **design** is the most important word. Design implies initiative, creativity, and personal agency. It emphasizes your own way of doing things, and your desire to shift the way you are living.

Spiritual practices can be studied and understood at an intellectual level, of course. **Yet the most important aspect is deciding to begin.** You create a new set of habits, get specific about what and when, establish some accountability, and set forth.

Practice repeats by definition, so you keep on with some measure of steady intention. Playing music, doing dance steps, working a basketball, knitting a blanket, are all repetitive actions. You get better at the work if you put in the time and commitment.

Evaluation improves how you practice. You keep breaking it down into new steps—week by week, month by month, year by year. Taking a *Spirit Journey* implies that design work is ongoing.

Reality check: There will be no graduation day into absolute harmony, balance, and perfect performance. There are peak days and there are days when it all falls apart. The boat which carries you in the waves of life gets stronger though, and that matters quite a bit. Spiritual practices are a beautiful tool kit you develop, a designed approach to living that involves new habits.

There is much research on forming habits which tells us what works:

- **Develop** a plan that is not too grandiose or overly rigorous as you embark.

- **Establish** a different pattern for three weeks or more to anchor the change.

- **Write** down what you plan to do and tell someone about it and seek support.

- **Evaluate** and course-correct every week.

- **Motivate** yourself with positive affirmation and gentle patience, rather than shame and blame about perceived failures.

Beginning your more focused spiritual practice is not necessarily about signing up for intense study and years of discipline. That is a path for some, yet not the general norm for most humans. You can discover simple ways to improve your current life design now. Celebrate that you are even thinking about it! You don't need to use mandated methods, intense effort, or tools that don't fit who you are.

I am going to suggest a very broad menu for you to consider gently. Start with your current life, take stock, then work gradually towards change over time. Small steps, steady progress, supportive allies who cheer you on. That's the way it works best, and as you notice and appreciate positive changes, you are motived to do more.

As Lao Tzu, the famous Taoist master said: *The journey of a thousand miles begins with a single step.*

You can truly get better at living well in the midst of disruption and change. **Build a better boat. Today is your day to begin.**

STEP TWO: Ponder motivations. Establish intentions.

CLEARING
Martha Postlethwaite

Do not try to save
the whole world
or do anything grandiose.
Instead, create
a clearing
in the dense forest
of your life
and wait there
patiently,
until the song
that is your life
falls into your own cupped hands
and you recognize and greet it.
Only then will you know
how to give yourself to this world
so worthy of rescue.

Why are you going to do this work to create new habits? Why choose this now?

You need to find positive reasons to truly develop new habits. Be honest about your motivations and start this work for yourself, not because of external pressures. Do some writing, thinking, or talking with another person to get clearer. Suggestions for reading: Richard Rohr, "*Four Shapes to Transformation,*" in *Oneing,* Vol. 5, No. 1; Hugh G. Byrne, *The Here-and-Now Habit,* and Rick Hanson, *Neuro Dharma: New Science, Ancient Wisdom, and Seven Practices of the Highest Happiness.*

Here are some possible intentions for spiritual practice:

• **Make Space:** As Martha Postlethwaite beautifully suggested in the poem provided: *Create a clearing in the dense forest of your life.* Live with more spaciousness, less busyness, and more breathing time. Listen more, speak less. Stop doing and cultivate being.

• **Focus:** Form habits and structures of attention. Work on mindful awareness. Intervene with your overactive mind. Be clear where you want to put your energy and time. Design a shorter list.

• **Inquire:** Make time, early morning or evening, to do some journaling and ask yourself some important questions.
What is your deepest longing for yourself and the world?
What do you yearn to be, have, or do?
Is your current way of life working for you?
If not, what is the cost of change?
What more would you imagine for yourself,
    if you allowed creative design?

• **Transform:** *A transformed person is a participatory, inclusive and generous self.* (Richard Rohr, "*Four Shapes to Transformation,*" in *Oneing,* Vol. 5, No. 1). This is about the intentional choice to make changes. Again, spend some time asking yourself questions and writing to discover your answers.

Are there aspects of your personality you would like to develop more fully?

Do you wish to explore new things and mix up your routine?

Are people giving you feedback that makes you want to change?

What do you choose to change?

• **Thrive:** Once you decide you want to make choices to change the way you are living, there are many ways you can seek transformation.

Improve your health

Sustain your own spirit so living has more joy.

Connect to Source and develop your spiritual life.

Have a greater impact in the areas that matter most to you.

Ponder your legacy and contribution to this world.

Live your fullest life while you are here.

STEP THREE: Broaden the menu. Find your practices.

Expand the idea of what spiritual practice might be and you encounter a world of possibilities. On the next page are many ways to begin a spiritual practice. There is no one right answer as we all are unique. Any of these examples, done with repetition, intention, and mindful awareness, cultivates practice. The way you do the activity is the key.

Use the following list, or feel free to find your own practices. Begin by noticing what you already do and commit to it more fully. Expand your menu choices and try out some different actions weekly. You may discover new ways to tend your own wholeness. You might encounter a larger Spirit and Presence.

Think of this endeavor as play and exploration, not rigid performance. Improvise and shift as needed. If you are engaged with the "why?" in mind, you will have more ease and delight.

SUGGESTIONS FOR DEVELOPING
A SPIRITUAL PRACTICE

- **Mindful movement:** Walking, running, rowing, swimming, yoga, tai chi, dance.

- **Stillness:** Meditation, prayer, silence, chanting, visual focus on symbol or art, breathwork.

- **Spiritual reading:** Poetry, sacred texts, cultural essays, inspiring blogs, books that guide or illuminate.

- **Creative arts:** Making or hearing music, drawing, painting, coloring, writing, crafts, sewing, knitting, cooking, performances (online), museums (online).

- **Sacred space:** Worship circles, rituals you design, home altar creation, labyrinths, community events, holy places.

- **Nature:** Connect indoors and outdoors. Explore parks, gardens, yards, rivers, oceans, plants, rocks, minerals, forests, and trees. View a sunrise or sunset. Travel to new landscapes in different regions (online or in person) and make places of return that you get to know well.

- **Companions:** Create planned interactions. Who are your people? Your animals? Your support system? Are you connecting? Make this happen with scheduling and intention. Cultivate more purposeful relationships and set aside time to do this regularly.

- **Technology fast:** Establish zones without any electronics. Complete screen stop. Give your brain, eyes, neurochemistry rest. What is it like to be a creature in the natural world, unplugged?

STEP FOUR: Create the container. Stir the pot.

Designing your spiritual practice is an effort to get clear, specific, and focused. The intentions can be lofty, yet nothing happens until we break it down into small steps. Don't be vague or general here, or you will soon drift from the effort. The simpler and more achievable it is, the better!

The first three weeks need to feel so easy, good, and natural that you are motivated by the joy of accomplishing the goals. You can build to more frequency, or decide to deepen practice and expand time, if you desire, later on.

No heroic discipline is necessary. If that is your tendency, one practice might be to inquire "why?" and consider steady, more moderate action.

1. **Choose three practices from the list beginning on page 208 to explore for one week, a mix of familiar and new.**

2. **Plan exactly when this will happen.** Example:

A thirty-minute walk, three times in the week, between 3–5 p.m., on Monday/Wednesday/Friday.

Create a home altar on Saturday from 10–11 a.m.

Go without technology for four hours on Monday morning.

3. **Declare your specific plan and intentions in writing.** Post this somewhere you will see it regularly. Return to this written commitment every day, which establishes neural pathways in the brain.

4. **Get a support partner and share your plan, in writing or out loud.** This is a key component! Don't skip this one or consider it optional, because habits change when we share intentions. Maybe your friend or partner would like to create their own plan and you can hold each other accountable.

5. Check in with that support partner on a set schedule. For example: you send an email twice, Tuesday and Thursday, to say you checked your goals. This works best if the person is also committing to a plan, and you can do reciprocal encouragement. Remember not to give up if you miss a goal or the week did not go as planned. Simply recommit anew the next day and begin again.

STEP FIVE: Notice what arises. Follow the flow.

Take the time to observe your spiritual practice plan as it evolves over the week. What is actually happening now?

At the end of each week, take some time to evaluate what worked, what didn't. Observe with honesty, and without hand-wringing, drama, and judgment. If you beat yourself up, you will most likely stop. This is an exploration, not a forced march.

Analyze what happened with your support partner: Was your plan too ambitious? Did you try something and just not like it? Did you mean to take an action and completely forget? All good.

Celebrate the week you lived and the efforts you made. Be grateful for what you learned and experienced. Truly congratulate yourself. Let's say you did 30% of what you intended. Hooray for that success!

Start again. Repeat. Repeat. Repeat. That's spiritual practice.

STEP SIX: Integrate experience. Transform over time.

Decide what to keep, what to let go, or what to add on for a new week cycle. Commit again, with self-encouragement and love.

It's most effective to keep a mix of familiar and new until you get your rhythm going. Increase from three practices per week when and if you are ready, yet be careful not to go too high in expectations. Committing to fifteen practices in one week is likely to overwhelm most of us.

It's often better to keep a steady pace than to flame out in one gigantic burst of enthusiasm. Yet this pacing is something that goes with your particular temperament, desire, and energy levels.

This is an open design process, a *Spirit Journey*. There is no way to fail or get it wrong, truly.

Explore the territory with kindness and a friendly heart.

Hold the "why?" as a North Star for guidance and motivation. Regularly assess how you may be changing, and where you might be headed next. Practice has seasons, and we don't need the exact same things over time. Sensing that your practices need to change is another signal that you may have inner work to discover and discern.

Keep going, stay steady, and get more practiced at navigating life and transformation!

Consider all the pain and all the pleasure
You have ever experienced
As waves on a very deep ocean which you are.

From the depths, witness those waves,
Rolling along so bravely, always changing.
Beautiful in their self-sustaining power.

Marvel that once, you identified with
Only the surface of this ocean.
Now embrace waves, depths, undersea mountains,
Out to the farthest shore.

—*The Radiance Sutras: 112 Gateways to the Yoga
   of Wonder & Delight,* Insight Verse 136, p. 150,
   translation by Lorin Roche

"The secret of living well is not in having all the answers
but in pursuing unanswerable questions in good company."
—Rachel Naomi Remen

WANT TO GO DEEPER
AND IN GOOD COMPANY?

Kathy Izard created Women|Faith & Story which is an online
community of leaders and learners who want to find what is calling them. We offer virtual interactive workshops encompassing
life coaching, spiritual direction, and creativity to help you on
your journey. Both Kathy and Louise offer workshops as well as
one-on-one coaching through Women|Faith & Story.

We hope you will join us.

WOMEN | FAITH & STORY

www.womenfaithstory.com
WF&S provides customized programs for groups and retreats.
Email us to design your program: Womenfaithstory@gmail.com
Follow WF&S on Instagram: @Womenfaithstory

LIKE THIS BOOK?

Reviews from readers like you help books like
The Last Ordinary Hour get discovered.

If you enjoyed this book, please consider
leaving a review on Amazon or Goodreads.
If you really loved it, write a review
and share a copy with a friend.

It is the best compliment you can give an author.

WANT TO TELL THE AUTHOR
WHAT YOU THOUGHT?

Readers can email Kathy Izard: kathy@kathyizard.com

Made in the USA
Columbia, SC
24 April 2023

15758156R00138